THE ABCs OF ENLIGHTENMENT

The ABCs of Enlightenment

A Memoir of Learning and Teaching

Robert Day

Serving House Books

The ABCs of Enlightenment:
A Memoir of Learning and Teaching

ISBN: 13:978-0-9971010-7-2

Cover and book design by Diane Landskroener
Serving House Books logo by Barry Lereng Wilmont

Published by Serving House Books
Copenhagen, Denmark and Florham Park, NJ
www.servinghousebooks.com

Member of The Independent Book Publishers Association
First Serving House Books Edition 2016

For all my teachers herein celebrated and for all the
students I have taught who learned from them
to pass on to others.

And Kathryn Jankus Day.

*What you leave behind is not what is engraved in stone
monuments, but what is woven into the lives of others.*
                                                    — Pericles

Also by Robert Day

Where I Am Now (stories)

The Committee to Save the World (literary nonfiction)

The Last Cattle Drive (a novel)

Speaking French in Kansas (stories)

We Should Have Come by Water (poems)

In My Stead (a novella)

Four Wheel Drive Quartet (a novella)

The Billion Dollar Dream (stories)

Chance Encounters of a Literary Kind (memoir)

Let Us Imagine Lost Love (a novel)

Robert Day for President (a campaign autobiography)

Contents

Publication Notes

Most of the "Learning" pieces were first published in the *University of Kansas Alumni Magazine*, having been written as *Gedenkshrifts* and *Festschrifts*. Most of the "Teaching" pieces were published in *The Washington Post Magazine* or *The Baltimore Sun*. That the author has not kept very good track of his bibliographical self gives him some curious pleasure (see "But Yet").

Preface

Reading these pieces over, I am struck by how much my "learning" as a student defined my "teaching" at Washington College and other colleges and universities as well. I learned because I was included in the process of learning: my best teachers brought me into their intellectual lives (see the "Foreword" to *Make Their Presence Known Wherever You Go: Tributes to Professors Carroll Edwards, Edmund Ruhe, Edgar Wolfe* by Robert Day and Fred Whitehouse). It seemed natural to do the same for my students, and in so doing, like my teachers, I joined what Borges called *el salón de estudiantes* instead of *el salón de profesores* even as a professor—especially as a professor.

However, I recall with some chagrin a moment with the Pulitzer Prize poet Gwendolyn Brooks, whom I had invited to Washington College to meet with students and give a reading at a local African American church (see Peter Turchi's "Afterword").

Miss Brooks (we used *Miss* in those days) had come into the Washington College's Rose O'Neill Literary House to have lunch with the student poets whose work she had read in advance and with whom she would be meeting in individual conferences later in the afternoon. By way of introduction to the assembled students I said to Miss Brooks, "These are my student poets." She paused, looked at them, turned to me and said, "Bob, they are not 'student poets'—they are 'poets' and they are not yours."

Of course.

Then there is my memory of being Charlton Hinman's student when he was one of the finest Shakespeare scholars in America. I had written the piece at the suggestion of Barbara Mowat when she learned I had studied with Hinman (see "Introduction") for submission to the *Shakespeare Quarterly,* where she had once been the editor and where she thought it might find a home. But the new editor had a problem: If he published it, he would be *inundated* with "Memories of My Favorite Shakespeare Professor" and, as there would be as many memories as Shakespeare professors, he had neither the staff nor the time to sift through them all.

However, sifting through my own history of who I became because teachers like Charlton Hinman saw in me someone worth their time has been a pleasure like none other I have had in my literary life.

— Robert Day

Introduction

When I first met Bob Day back in the mid-1980s, I was the newly appointed Dean of Washington College and Bob was the most unlikely English Professor I had ever met. The students loved him, and many came to the College in order to be in his classes and workshops; he was a wonderful writer—I'll never forget my first reading of *The Last Cattle Drive*—and he was clearly a good friend to his colleagues, and, in his own way, a dedicated member of the College faculty. But he stood apart—not from the students, but from everyone and everything else. He was a truth-teller, seemingly untouched by the academy. At the time, I guess I thought him a self-made man.

During my stay at Washington College, I had no idea Bob and I shared anything other than our love of literature, of learning, and of "the College." In recent years, though, we've discovered that just as he had studied with the great Shakespeare scholar Charlton Hinman, I had studied with Fredson Bowers, who had been Hinman's teacher. Surely when we were students, neither of us knew how blessed we were to learn from these giants, scholars who focused on Shakespeare's words and on how those words had come down to us by way of sixteenth- and seventeenth-century compositors and printers. My study with Bowers had a direct influence on my own career; Bob's study with Hinman (see "But Yet") reveals itself more subtly, I think, in

Bob's love of words—the words that make up literary works of art, and the words he takes such pleasure in finding as he crafts his own poetry-like prose. I feel that Hinman is also strongly present in the joy Bob finds in letterpress printing. (See "Print It As It Stands: Beautifully," and, especially, "Tales Out of School.")

After reading the essays collected in this memoir, I no longer think of Bob Day as a self-made man. That self-making, I now know, was strongly mediated not only by Hinman but by several other of his professors back at the University of Kansas, each of whom is, in his telling, "my teacher." From them he learned devotion to literature—its craft and the culture it carries with it; he learned about teaching as a vocation (in the purist sense of that word); and he learned that the life of the mind is infinitely more important than anything else—except for one's students. He saw in his teachers a love of their subject matter so strong that it had to be shared—with him and with other students. He saw in his teachers' faces an incredible dignity, "as if [they had been] wounded by what they'd seen near the bone of *King Lear* . . . or Mahler's *Ninth*" ("Parts of Their Night"). From them he learned about the magic of the imagination, of the love for story (see "Solempe"). Thus, when he speaks of "a good and generous education" ("Famous Education"), of "those important conversations we call teaching" ("Tales Out of School"); when he says to students (in "The ABCs of Enlightenment") that "Language is lovely. The history of language is inexhaustibly lovely"; when (in "Tales Out of School") he thus recalls his meeting with a student: "He

4

wants me to be his teacher….What I have to do is figure out how to let him learn"—these are all moments when those professors who figured out how to let the young Bob Day learn are, through Bob, continuing to speak, continuing to share.

This might make Bob Day sound a bit soft, a bit sentimental. Nothing could be farther from the truth. Anger lies just beneath the surface of his writing about present-day education. Read his "The Myth of Good Teaching," where "the myth" is that "good college classroom teaching [has] any value in the academic marketplace." What can be done about that? he asks. Not much. "There is of course satisfaction in itself from teaching well; not unlike the pleasure of learning is the pleasure of learning—thus a liberal arts education, also not a valued currency." Clear-sighted amusement lies just next to the anger. Enjoy, for example, his devastatingly comic self-descriptions, as when (in "Tales of Retirement") the lovely young student wants to give him a hug. "Me?" I said, standing straighter while trying to deflate my inner-tube girth. "Me?" "Yes," she said. … "It's just that you remind me so much of my grandfather." Or see the anger and the amusement merge, as when (in "Allen Ginsberg Levitates Chestertown") Ginsberg "wanted to levitate some of the buildings, both on campus and off. 'Sure,' I said. The dean had recently admonished the faculty to provide 'unique educational experiences' for our students, and I thought: a building levitation might look good on my annual report."

These are delightful essays. I especially love "We'll Always Have McSorley's," "I Look Out for Ed Wolfe," and "Tales Out of School." I've come away from reading them feeling immense gratitude to those lovely men back in Kansas who saw in Bob Day a worthy recipient of their care and attention. And I'm grateful to Bob Day for crafting these pieces for our delectation.

— Barbara Mowat

LEARNING

Foreword to LEARNING

The professors whose tributes appear in these pages shaped the lives of thousands of students at the University of Kansas from the 1950s and the decades beyond. They did so because those of us who enrolled in their courses saw in them a commitment to a life of the mind that was theirs with pleasure and grace. They were superb scholars and writers and teachers because they had discovered in their studies of literature what Vladimir Nabokov called "aesthetic bliss": of craft, of language, of character, of plot, of design—plus the delight and instruction by the literary cultures of previous centuries—and it was not possible for them to keep their affections for what they had learned to themselves. They had to tell someone. And so they told us, their students.

Ed Ruhe, Carroll Edwards, and Edgar Wolfe did not have academic "careers"; they were not "*dangerous committee men*"—to steal a line from Howard Nemerov; they did not "network" at "conferences"; they did not watch television (with one notable exception: Ed Ruhe rented a television so he could watch with glee the Watergate hearings). Were they alive today, they would not have cell phones; they would not Text; they would not have pages on My Face; they would not Twitter. Unto themselves they were a community of learning into which we were invited to share the pleasures of the life of their minds, and ours as well.

Those of us who studied with them understood that when you left their classrooms, you never left their classrooms.

— Robert Day

Parts Of Their Night

He never seemed to know what kind of car he owned nor what sports season it was. On the other hand, he always seemed to know what nasty business Richard Nixon was up to, or what new Bergman film was being released.

When I first met him in 1959, it was football season and he drove a rusting blue 1952 wrap-around-windshield, four-door Pontiac. I remember the car not only because as a freshman from the suburbs you knew everything about cars in those days, but because Professor Ruhe—for that's who he was to me as the teacher of my freshman English class—and I had spent nearly an hour late one afternoon trying to find the auto in question before it quietly dawned on him that he'd walked to campus that day.

"Maybe it's in the parking lot by the football stadium," I recall saying about halfway through the search.

"*Virgin Spring* is playing this evening," Professor Ruhe said by way of response. "Eight p.m. showing. I hope they don't cut it."

Why he had offered me a ride home after our class, I don't remember. I do remember that I could have gotten back to my dorm under my own steam in plenty of time for supper, but now the matter seemed in doubt. Hunger in a young man is never metaphysical. Still, out of some kind of respect that is difficult to name these days, in the 1950s you didn't abandon a professor in search of his car—no matter how much your stomach growled.

By now we'd walked through three KU parking lots, down two side streets, and were heading more or less at random across the campus lawns toward the campanile and, beyond the duck pond, my dorm. Our search was apparently not along the horizontal and vertical grid you use when on patrol for lost Boy Scouts; instead we seemed to be going over a landscape of verbal paths in Professor Ruhe's mind, some set of associations that formed a map all its own. On these cerebral walkways we'd already come upon Blake and Johnson, taken a left turn out of the parking lot at Pope and Swift, and trudged up a hill toward Hardy and Ernest Dowson. It was near the campanile that we came upon Bergman, *Virgin Spring*, and Richard Nixon.

Here and there a few students were walking toward the student union for supper. In the distance a brass pep band was blaring a fight song. The afternoon was gold turning to red. Across the duck pond I could see my dorm: a stacked hotel of square windows.

"What color is your car?" I asked; I was on the lunatic fringe of starvation. Early on he had told me we were looking for "something General Motors." Years later, after I was no longer his student and had become his friend, I watched in placid amazement as—with the certainty of a stockbroker getting into his Silver Bullet Porsche—he climbed into a car he had sold two years before only to be foiled in his attempt to drive it off because his "something Japanese" keys would not fit the lock of his previously owned "something Ford."

"Green," he said. "Green."

"Green?" I said.

"Blue," he said.

"Blue?" I said.

"I suppose they'll cut it badly," he said. I had no idea what he was talking about.

"Yes," I said.

"It's Richard Nixon's tribe at work again," he said. And here Professor Ruhe shook his head, pursed his lips and let loose something like a rumble of distant thunder. Over the years those of us who became his friends knew that sound as the precursor to an inevitable rant about one of his permanent angers: censorship, materialism, suburban ethics, Richard Nixon, teacher-evaluation forms, and what he called "the corporate university." The disgust of ancient free thinkers seemed to echo in his thunder; the dismay of American civil libertarians shook with his head. It was as if he might keep such nonsense at bay with contempt and derision. He was largely an innocent man.

"James Agee," he said after a moment as we stood there in the bulging shadows of the campus buildings that were turning the afternoon into evening. "James Agee wrote that official acceptance is a sure sign of fatal misunderstanding. And Mozart wrote that he'd spent his life searching for notes that loved one another." We learned that our professor's rant could be calmed by a self-administered dose of James Agee or Mozart, not to mention hundreds of other splendid authors, painters and composers who formed the matrix of his life and were a delight and balm to his soul. A little Mozart went a long way in his various battles with Richard Nixon.

"What do you think?" he asked me.

I was eighteen. I was from the suburbs. I didn't know

James Agee or Bergman or Blake or Johnson or *Virgin Spring*— whoever she was. I knew how to throw a curve ball to the outside corner of the plate and how to set a pick for a cutting guard; I knew Ozzie and Harriet were married off television as well as on; and I knew that General Eisenhower had been president of the United States since the beginning of real time. It was 1959. Football fall, 1959. We all had a lot to learn. We were all largely innocent. I didn't know what to think.

* * *

"Hello," he says. It is decades later. Ed Ruhe—for that is who he is to me now— Ed Ruhe has answered the phone in that half-hectic voice we who were his students know.

"*The Atlantic Monthly* calling," I say. He plays along.

"What can I do for you?"

"We need a piece on Richard Nixon as the emblem of ethics in government," I say. "Five thousand words."

"I can't even get to five hundred words," he says through his laugh. "Like a freshman blue book." In my mind's eye I can see his head shaking in the old wrath; then it stops. I ask him how he is.

"Fine," he says. "I've been thinking about Flannery O'Connor. And you?"

"I've been thinking about William Stafford's poetry," I say.

"How firm and sure it is," he says. "'Pray for the frozen dead at Yellow Knife/These words we send are becoming parts of their night.'"

"Yes," I say.

"I've been thinking about the revelations in O'Connor," he says. "Those visions."

"Astounding, aren't they?" I say.

We are silent for a moment because he needs to catch his breath. I find myself thinking about teachers: good teachers, bad teachers, great teachers. It's a television topic these days. But I am thinking that my best teachers were always a bit zany around the social edges and no doubt maladjusted at the core, as if wounded by what they'd seen near the bone of *King Lear*, "The Rhyme of the Ancient Mariner," *The Seventh Seal*, or Mahler's *Ninth*. These professors all had something I think of as dignity. How this grew out from their character and into their physiognomy and fixed me with its authority I am sure I know: They loved their teaching subjects above all else, and it showed. It showed on Ed Ruhe more than most.

"Remember those teacher-evaluation forms the students filled out on you?" I say.

"They wrote I had annoying personal mannerisms," he says. I hear faint thunder. Absurdly, I am recalling the time he taped Rilke poems to the dashboard of his car so he could learn German as he drove around town. We watched him motor through stop signs on his way to fluency.

"What are you reading?" I ask.

"Joyce Cary," he says. "You know we never gave Bill Stafford an honorary degree. What madness is that?"

"He doesn't have any oil wells," I say.

"Poets don't have oil wells," he says. "We have to do better."

"I think we do," I say.

It occurs to me that over the years most of our battles have been lost, but I don't say this. Instead we trade a few stories: It is the pleasure of good friends, this telling of the same tales over and over again as if by so doing we can weave a tapestry against mortality.

"I've been watching *Walkabout*," he says. "And practicing my colloquial language."

"What colloquial language?"

"You know," he says, "how the students complained on my evaluations that I didn't speak their language, so I'm practicing: 'Milton uses epic similes, man! Sam Johnson is the English Dictionary, wow, really! Blake gets in your face, man!'"

"You'll be the teacher of the decade," I say. "You'll get an award. Official acceptance."

Again a moment of silence while he catches his breath, then laughs.

"I've got to go," he says. Through the phone I hear that someone has come into the back of his apartment, perhaps a former student like myself. We stop in on him these days.

"See you later," I say.

"You know what Auden said?" he asks.

"What?"

"That talk about literature should be filled with insight and advocacy. What do you think?"

"Auden's right," I say. I am thinking of Bill Stafford's poems, of James Agee, of notes that love one another, of Lear, of insight and advocacy, of visions, and of walks you take in your life with Johnson and Milton and Bergman as companions. Before he hangs up, Ed asks me to remember him to some former students.

"I've got to go," he says.

"Goodbye," I say.

"Goodbye," he says.

Goodbye: So say we all.

Solempe

Above all Carroll Edwards liked language and stories, which meant that he was an especially gifted professor of Chaucer. "Think of words in *The Canterbury Tales* that you like better than the words we use today," he'd say to his students. This was usually followed by more than a moment of silence in the classroom. "Can't think of any? How about *drugge*? Or *miswent*. Or *rewde*." More silence. "Still none of your own?

"Well," he would say, "then as you read Our Chaucer"—Chaucer was always "Our Chaucer" to Professor Edwards, as if the great English poet were writing away in the back of John Fowler's Abington Book Shop or at a table in the Gaslight Tavern next door, or perhaps at the Jayhawk Café down the street—"as you read Our Chaucer find for yourself his words that you like better than your words. *Rewde* instead of ignorant. *Drugge* for labor. Keep a list. I have mine." And here Professor Edwards would tap his head and then note that as a boy in Colorado he had been a catcher for a local baseball team, but because his family was too poor to buy him a glove he caught fastball pitchers barehanded: "*Hond*" he would say, holding up his ungloved hand. "And isn't *miswent* just the right word for what it means?"

The first word I chose was *Aprille* because I had in those days a girlfriend named April who from then on—and much to her amusement— became Aprille. You stress the *rille*. It was later that I learned *solempe* meant "special dignity."

As to the stories from "Our Chaucer," Professor Edward's favorite was probably "The Wife of Bath's Tale," which he would narrate in class, complete with a moral of his own for a coda. If the literary students in those days got wind of the telling, they would crowd into Edwards' classroom and stand along the sides or sit in the window ledges in back (there were never any empty seats in Carroll Edwards' courses) to hear it.

After everyone settled down, and after Professor Edwards closed his Chaucer book and put his elbows on the table and—via some medieval form of magical realism—began to acquire the physiognomy of Our Chaucer, he would commence his version of the story complete with personal embellishments along the way—as well as nods to the men in attendance. By my memory it went like this:

"A young Knight of the Round Table—not unlike some of you handsome fraternity boys in this class—was a bit too rapacious with a woman on the edge of a Kansas wheat field, and King Arthur decided to behead you for your transgression. But Guinevere took a liking to our Knight and suggested to Arthur that he send you on a mission to find out what women most desire. King Arthur thought that he might like to know that himself and so a deal was cut: If you found the answer to what women most desire, your life would be spared. If not, not. In any case, you were honor-bound to return to face your fate. You had a year and a day."

And here Professor Edwards would pause and look around the room as if to say, Should anyone know the answer to what it is women most desire, we can stop the story here and now. In the class I attended, no one said a thing.

"So off you went the world over and heard many ideas about what women most desire (flattery, diamonds as big as the Ritz, Mercedes convertibles) but none of the answers seem right, and so it was with your 'wagon dragging' (we thought this might be an expression from Professor Edwards' youth in rural Colorado) you started back to have your head lopped off."

Again a pause. All the men—now absorbed into the tale—were deeply curious. As were the women, some of them no doubt dating the men who were about to either get the answer right or lose their heads.

"As fate would have it, on the day before our Knight is to return, he passes a Witch of a Hag in the woods stirring her pot. She sees him and wonders why he is so gloomy. He tells her his tale—that tomorrow he will lose his life because he has not discovered what women most desire. The Hag says she will tell him the answer if he will marry her; you agree, and another deal is cut. She is very ugly and very old. We must remember this. Very ugly."

Again a pause. Silence.

"At court the next day Guinevere asks the Knight what it is that women most desire, and he cocks his ear toward the wizen Hag and she tells him something at which he smiles, and he in turn says, 'It is *sovereignty* that women most desire.' Guinevere smiles. Arthur smiles. The Knight smiles. The Hag smiles broadly."

And here Professor Edwards would look around the

room to see if any of us are smiling. I don't know what he saw, but before he continued, Professor Edwards smiled. Broadly.

"Well, a great celebration is about to begin because the Knight's life will be spared, but the old Hag says, 'Wait a moment! That young fraternity man you sent on the quest to find out what women most desire promised he'd marry me if I got the answer right.' Guinevere wants to know if this is true, and the Knight confesses it is, but protests that the Hag is ... well, a hag and very old and ugly. Very ugly. The protest is overruled and the marriage takes place, and you and your Witch of a Hag of a Wife head back to her pad for your wedding night."

There is a long silence in the classroom while we contemplate this.

"Now it is evening and the Knight and the Hag are in bed and he's sleeping on his stomach, not wanting to be bothered. However, the Hag pokes him and wants to know the problem, because she is ready for a night of carnal pleasure, and the Knight says, 'Well, you're old and ugly and being in bed with you—much less married to you—is not what I had in mind for a night of carnal pleasure.'"

—OK, she says, how about we cut a deal?

—What kind of deal?

—I will change myself into a beautiful young woman with firm breasts and long legs, but as such I might be unfaithful to you. Or I can stay as I am, and always be true.

—How can you change yourself into a beautiful young woman? asks the Knight.

—By magic, says the Witch of a Hag of a Wife.

"After a moment it occurs to our Knight that he has learned something at court earlier that day, and so he says to his wife: 'You may be whatever you want to be.' And with that the Hag turns herself into a beautiful and eternally young woman who will remain forever faithful."

Silence. Somehow we sense Professor Edwards is not finished even though Our Chaucer is. Then:

"The moral is that many of you think that such women exist only by magic."

* * *

When Fred Whitehead told me Carroll Edwards had died I said I'd fly back for the parade.

"What parade?" Fred said.

"Won't there be a parade in his honor? Literary students and English department faculty dressed up as characters of *The Canterbury Tales*: The Miller. The Knight. The Merchant. The Pardoner. The Wife of Bath. I can see it now. We'll assemble at the Chi Omega fountain: The Cook with his open sore. Aprille as Alisoun. The Chaucer Professor will be the Narrator and read from the "Prologue" as we march through campus, making stops along the way. Snow Hall. Strong Hall. Green Hall. The Gaslight Tavern. The Abington Book Shop. At each stop one of the characters will read a passage from his or her tale until we assemble at the Rock Chalk Café as if it were the Cathedral at Canterbury. Then we'll recite our words: *Queme, Digne, Auctour, Solempe*. And more. All in honor of Carroll Edwards. I want to be Nicholas. Who do you want to be?"

Fred is silent. Finally.

"Bob, the Gaslight Tavern and the Abington Book Shop are now parking lots; the Rock Chalk Cathedral is a condominium/hotel. And such parades exist only by magic."

I Look Out For Ed Wolfe

Being Twelve Notes on the Craft of Fiction, University Days, Coincidence, The Mind's Eye, Significant Details, Multiple Sclerosis, One Teacher Plus One Character from Fiction, All on a Snowy Winter Afternoon in a Now Defunct Campus Building, and Written With Correct Spelling and Punctuation, plus a Modicum of Sentimentality for Which the Author Does Not Apologize.

1. The Nature of Titles. The Nature of Coincidence.

One of the things I learned from Ed Wolfe, my writing professor, is that you can't copyright titles. I could have called this essay "Of Education," or "War and Peace," or "Thirteen Ways of Looking at a Blackbird." I could have called it "Penny Lane"—a song that was popular during the years I learned about titles and other literary matters from a man whose name happened to be Ed Wolfe—as in the famous short story by Stanley Elkin, "I Look Out for Ed Wolfe."

Coincidence, my Ed Wolfe will teach his students, is one of the energies of fiction. It turned out my Ed Wolfe and Stanley Elkin meet each other one sad day, and that years later I meet Stanley Elkin on another sad day; these coincidences are the rough stuff of life, but more on that later. For now, back to the present/past: You were first in print, Mr. Elkin, but I hereby exercise my muse-given right to be a literary thief. I, too, looked out for Ed Wolfe.

2. An Old Campus Building. Harris Flora and John Donne.

I am sitting in Fraser Hall, now defunct, the victim of some dreary university administration that thought it would look better as a pile of rocks than as the aging ivy twin tower building it was—and still is in my imagination, where I have held both Ed Wolfe and his Fraser Hall office like a hologram against a practical and efficient world. Imagine the specifics of the objects you are describing, Ed Wolfe will teach me. Imagine them in detail.

Part of whatever ability I have to express what I imagine about such places as Fraser Hall I owe to Ed Wolfe. It is not enough to have talent, he has told me (although he's never told me I have talent), and it is not enough to want to be a writer (although he knows I want to accomplish that)—what I need is duty to the craft. And patience with myself would help. (I have told him at our previous meeting if I don't get published in *The New Yorker* by the time I am twenty-two, I'm going to stop writing and take up a job as the sheriff of Two Sleeps, Wyoming.) And finally, Ed Wolfe will note again: An eye for detail is where honesty in fiction rests.

Beyond these lessons, Ed Wolfe suggests I might also want to do plenty of reading. Long before Saul Bellow made his famous remark, Ed Wolfe has been teaching his students that writers should be readers moved to emulation. Learn to write dialogue from Ring Lardner, Ed Wolfe has said to me. Since I'd never heard of Ring Lardner I kept my mouth shut and later bought a Scribner's copy of *Haircut and Other Stories*. My library of books as texts to learn the craft of writing grows larger than my literary course library. It is a good beginning.

Ed Wolfe, like E. M. Forster before him, thought of literary tradition not so much as a historical queue of English authors, but rather as a round dinner table where we all ate together and talked books.

Pull up a chair, Mr. Donne and Miss Austen. That's Bob Day and Harris Flora sitting across from you. Why don't you read your work aloud and talk. Mr. Day, Mr. Flora, you listen and learn. It is through such *en famille* literary meals that I have begun the process of becoming a writer.

By the time I am sitting across from Ed Wolfe in Fraser Hall this singular snowy winter afternoon, I have read my Ring Lardner. As well, I have learned from Katherine Anne Porter, William Stafford, J. D. Salinger, Jack London, Vladimir Nabokov, Ed Wolfe, Robert Service, and Jane Austen.

Harris Flora, my friend and fellow student writer in those days, has been instructed to learn from John Dos Passos, Sherwood Anderson, and the English novelist George Meredith. Harris and I have been trading what we have learned over lunch at the Gaslight Tavern. Ed Wolfe is teaching us how to teach ourselves: He knows that; we don't. It is called dramatic irony.

3. God Knows We Are All Unbearably Sentimental.

God knows we are all unbearably sentimental about our college education. Our American minds are full of guitar songs, wine bottles with candles in them, used Studebakers, the back seats of used Studebakers, good friends past and forgotten with the rest, campus dogs and ducks, and the hallways and staircases of old stone buildings. I sometimes wonder how the chairs and benches of our college memories can be sat upon at all as they seem so precious and painterly.

Was Fraser Hall really all that worn and splendid? And my teacher, Ed Wolfe? Is he as instructive as this memoir makes him out to be? Or are they both wasted space: a campus building that when you cut away large swatches of the ivy on its sides reveals to the prying eyes of the engineer witch doctors (who knew "it" all along) "significant" cracks placidly making their way among the stones; and what of Ed Wolfe, an "Associate" Professor (remember Elizabeth Taylor nagging Richard Burton in *Who's Afraid of Virginia Woolf*: "Associate Professor, Associate Professor") with but one novel published, no Ph.D., and a slow and deliberate fashion of speech that is at odds with the impatient generation he is teaching? What to make of the long pauses between your questions and his answers? What to the prying eyes of academic-promotion engineers does Ed Wolfe reveal?

4. Mecurical, Mercurial and Nina Wolfe.

Ed Wolfe's office slants toward the east exterior wall of the building, and when you visit him you sit in the only other chair in the room—a swivel chair of the professor whose desk is near the door but who is seldom there. The chair you sit in, the desk where you sit, the book shelves that rise up the wall in front of the desk, all combine to give you a feeling of importance: It is the seed of pretentiousness, and it is difficult when you are nineteen and have the week before just written your first really long story—it is difficult not to swivel and rock back in your office chair, as if you were debating in your mind the influence of Hemingway's work on your own.

Ed Wolfe does not seem to notice: He points out you've yet to spell "suburban" correctly, and that it took "both of them" (by which he means that his wife, Nina, who is bedridden with multiple sclerosis, has been consulted) to understand that "mecurical" was "mercurial." And then there are some matters of punctuation. Is it impossible for me to learn where in a quoted question the question mark is to be placed? So much for Hemingway.

5. Cornucopia Finance Corporation and the *Mind's Eye*.

The Ed Wolfe that Stanley Elkin looks out for is a telephone-bill collector who loses his job because he's too aggressive in collecting his accounts for Cornucopia Finance Corporation.

"You're in trouble. It means a lien. A judgment. We've got lawyers. You've got nothing. We'll pull the furniture the hell out of there. The car. Everything . . . If you're short, grow. This is America." His boss fires him.

Stanley Elkin's Ed Wolfe takes his severance pay, adds some money from selling his clothes and car, and empties his checking and savings accounts so that added together his net worth is $2,479.03—all of which he accumulates in cash with the idea of making it through the rest of his life. In the end, Elkin's Ed Wolfe throws it all away: One night both life and money get tossed onto the damp dirty floor of a dreary tavern. So much for the American Dream.

Stanley Elkin's Ed Wolfe and my Ed Wolfe have little in common: True, they both play handball (my Ed Wolfe was a champion), but beyond that, nothing. Still, there is something magical about their mere coincidental existence, if not their antithesis; it is as if all concerned (the two Eds and the two authors) have conspired to make fiction fluctuate between reality and the hologram of the mind's eye—between the real snow I see falling outside my Ed Wolfe's office window and the snow we see in the glass ball of winter scenes.

6. Wallace Stevens and Snow.

Fraser Hall is old and drafty, a firetrap, and full of wasted space. "Wasted space" was a great sin to the university administrators who never bothered to look out their windows at the broad sweep of prairie around them.

Looking out of Ed Wolfe's office window I can see east 20 miles down the Kansas River Valley toward Eudora and Kansas City. Even in the huge brush strokes of the panorama I can see the details of small farming roads and teardrop-shaped ponds among the larger lovely space. It is blue outside. Blue and gray and white. It is winter; it is snowing. And, as Wallace Stevens has predicted in a previous class, it is going to snow.

7. Some Events Narrated Out of Sequence.

Because he cares for his wife with the same combination of duty and affection that he cares for words, Ed Wolfe knows a great deal about multiple sclerosis. At some point Ed Wolfe meets Stanley Elkin, the unwitting author of "I Look Out For Ed Wolfe." At that meeting Ed Wolfe notices certain symptoms in Stanley Elkin (having to do with the eyes) that are precursors to multiple sclerosis. Ed Wolfe tells Stanley Elkin what he knows.

Years later in San Francisco I meet Stanley Elkin in a hotel lobby. I do not know the story about Ed Wolfe telling Stanley Elkin what he has told him. Nor of its prophetic truth. I say: "My teacher was Ed Wolfe at the University of Kansas. Do you know him?"

"Yes," says Stanley Elkin, and when he gets up to greet me I see that he has a cane and that he is shaking. "He was my teacher too." Mr. Elkin sits back down and looks to his left as if searching for a window out of which he can stare.

I do not know what any of this means, but I sense I have walked into an office where I should not be. I back away without saying anything more. It would be much later that I learn this part of the story.

8. What I Am Writing.

I am writing these sentences to discover what I think about these matters, just as I am sitting in Ed Wolfe's office to discover what I have written. There are forty years between my two selves. By what name is that space to be called. If it is a question, should I try to answer it?

9. The Sentimental Education of Young Writers at the Gaslight Tavern.

In those days, before the boom in college Creative Writing Programs and all the modern techniques that go with them, which, I want to confess up front, I am as responsible as the next writer/teacher of spreading, you learned your craft not so much from "the writing program" as from your teacher—and you learned writing not so much in the classroom as from the other end of the log. In Ed Wolfe's case this process began when he returned your story— usually a week or so after you had turned it in. What you got back was an annotated edition of your work with a long handwritten survey of its accomplishments and faults.

The survey would start on the back of your final page and proceed from your story's conclusion toward your story's beginning. You'd find Ed Wolfe's account was complete with samples of what you might have written; whole sections of your story would be reworked, complete with dialogue and narration. Often when you'd turn your story's pages over from Ed Wolfe's writing to yours, you'd discover that his comments matched page for page the very text he was rewriting. It was a twice-told tale, and it was enormously flattering. For reasons I cannot explain, this process did not violate your sense of artistic honor—which at nineteen could easily be violated in a thousand small ways.

Harris Flora and I would take our Ed Wolfe/Flora/Day stories to the Gaslight Tavern and read aloud what we had written. Is it to our credit (I think it is) that we wondered then if energy for Ed Wolfe's own fiction was being spent on ours, that for every sentence he rewrote for us, he used up a sentence he might have written for himself? It was the kind of simple equation you believe in when you are young and talking about literature and drinking beer. What does it say about me that I believe it even now?

At the end of Ed Wolfe's survey you'd get your grade and a small drawing of a wolf. Well, sort of a wolf. It was a most benign wolf, and it seemed to have been drawn out of the very script that Ed Wolfe used to critique your work, almost as if the letters that might have gone into yet another rewritten sentence had found themselves rearranged into a modest-size drawing of a mildly amused and harmless wolf, teeth and all.

10. The Slant of Ed Wolfe's Office. The Nature of Fiction. Duty.

The desk chair where I am sitting in Ed Wolfe's office has wheels, and over the course of your conversation with Ed Wolfe you have a tendency to roll downhill toward him, which turns out to be necessary because the longer Ed Wolfe talks, the softer he speaks. The important criticisms worthy of a good story are put very softly near the end of your conversation, so it is a good sign if by the end of your meeting you wind up more or less bumping chairs with Ed Wolfe. It is a bad sign if you don't spend enough time in the chair to slide very far downhill. Your progress down the slope of Ed Wolfe's Fraser Hall office is a barometer of how well you have written. This afternoon I won't make much progress toward the window where my teacher is framed in the fading light.

"I have decided," Ed Wolfe says, "to return to an old system of reading your stories." Here he holds up the front page of my work. I can see even in the gathering darkness (the office lights seemed never to be turned on) that my great opening scene is heavily penciled. Ed Wolfe turns the story around to show me that there is nothing written on the back of the final page. That is not a good sign at all. The longer the critique of your work, like the longer the roll you make in the office, the better your story is. One page of rewriting is no compliment at all. There was that folklore/rumor about the student who wrote so badly that Ed Wolfe wrote nothing in return. In the gloom of Ed

Wolfe's office I am beginning to feel like someone who has become a character in a fiction not of his own making.

"You need," Ed Wolfe says, "to have some respect for the spelling of the English language and the punctuation of English sentences. I have corrected the first page. I have not read further. You can correct the rest. When you have, return the story to me and we shall talk." He hands me my story and leans back in his chair and puts his left elbow on the window ledge.

Oddly, I notice for the first time that at the edge of window along the sill there is snow blowing in: A small drift is collecting just where Ed Wolfe's elbow is resting. I am wondering if I will ever be able to use in my writing what I am seeing: how to describe this thin, light crescent of snow assembling itself inside the window of a professor's office? How to match that up against the feeling of the weight my story makes in my hands as I realize there is a lifetime of work to do and yet I don't know what a lifetime of anything means?

"Words," Ed Wolfe says, leaning away from the window, "words are the first element in writing to admire. There are other things to admire about writing. Sentences. Plot. Character. But you must start with an affection for words." He pauses and turns his chair away from me so that we are both looking out his window. "What are you saying about a word when you don't bother to know how to spell it? What are you saying about a word if you abbreviate it? 'Cinn. M.S.' If you do that, who's to say if you'll describe anything correctly? Or admire the fullness of it? The snow outside my window. The different colors of shadows. The way the snow comes in through the crack and onto the sill." He turns back to face me. "The first details of fiction are words."

11. Questions of Fiction in Search of an Answer.

Suburban, mercurial. The crescent of snow along the edge of the window. The hologram in my mind of Fraser Hall that is lit only by the dimming afternoon light coming through Ed Wolfe's window. The glee and sorrow of coincidence. The flux of life and fiction. The Gaslight Tavern. Harris Flora. Ed Wolfe. Ed Wolfe. Stanley Elkin. The table where we all sit, words and question marks alike pulling up chairs along with Ring Lardner and John Donne and asking out loud, how do we know one another? And what will become of our fellowship? What indeed? If that is a question, do I have to answer it? I think I do. Even if it takes a lifetime of work.

12. "I Look Out for Ed Wolfe," a short story by Stanley Elkin.

I look out for Ed Wolfe.

But Yet

The year is 1964. The scene is a large office on the first floor of old Fraser Hall (now defunct) at the University of Kansas. The man sitting at his desk is framed in morning light and lawn by the campus behind him. His name is Professor Charlton Hinman, and, among the literary lessons I learned from him was that Shakespeare did not always observe the classical unities of time, place, and (about-to-come) action. *But yet...*

The door to Professor Hinman's office was usually closed; however, he had told his students they were welcome, just knock. We had developed a story about him (one among many) that he liked the flourishes that opening doors created. *Yes, come in, please*, you would hear him say in a baritone not (yet) diminished by his smoking (was it a pipe, or cigarettes?) *Yes, do come in and take a chair*, he would say, and curiously enough, stand to greet you, as if you were more important because you were one of his students than was he, being your professor. I walk in and sit down.

In those days Professor Hinman taught only seminars, and the rude rumor was that he did so because he was a poor teacher in large lecture halls. Not that anyone I knew had ever taken a lecture course from him, nor did my friends know anyone, nor...and so it went: campus folklore.

And it was also folklore that his celebrated seminar on Shakespeare's tragedies was by invitation only. While this prerequisite had made its way to the gossip among the student writers drinking our tomato beers at the Gaslight Tavern just off campus, it has not stopped me from being in Professor Hinman's office this morning because of my impertinence to attend the first meeting of the seminar with an "Add" slip for him to sign. Which he did. As result, we are to talk about *King Lear*.

"Now, Mr. Day, is it?" Professor Hinman says as he sits down, checks his appointment book, then gets out a single sheet of paper on which I had the week before typed three questions (Professor Hinman is to pick one) for me to address on my final exam toward the end of April. He studies the list, puffs his pipe (or takes a drag on a Camel), leans back, then forward.

"Mr. Day, is it?"

"Yes."

There is a phone on a table near the window behind him; soon it is going to ring.

Among the stories about Professor Hinman was that he had been a bombardier in World War II (in one version, he was the bombardier on the *Enola Gay*), and it occurred to him later, when he was at the University of Virginia or Johns Hopkins (as a student, a professor? And we were never sure if there was an "s" on John or not), it occurred to him…that…what? Well, we were not sure what, but it had something to do with looking through the Norden bombsight, but instead of seeing Hiroshima, Professor Hinman was looking at Quartos or Folios, or First Quartos or First Folios or Bad Quartos—but to what purpose those of us at the Gaslight Tavern never quite understood. We did, however, understand he was a famous Shakespeare scholar of a special kind: a Textual Scholar. And again, we were not sure what that meant; only it must mean something about the footnotes he used, never among them *ibid* or *ff*. Remember, we were not only the kin of Falstaff at the Gaslight, we were trying to be writers at the expense of being English majors.

Then there was Professor Hinman's wife, Mrs. Hinman. She had been a friend of Hemingway's in Paris. She had known James Joyce. There were photographs of her (not that we had seen them) inside Shakespeare and Company, where she had surely met Professor Hinman. Maybe Professor Hinman knew Joyce. Or Ezra Pound. My private hope was that he had seen Josephine Baker dance.

In any case, Mrs. Hinman (she never had a first name to us) could be seen on campus, a milkmaid of a certain age (always wearing aquamarine) with a braid wrapped around the top of her head for a hairdo. She looked like an elegant version of Gertrude Stein. If anyone in Lawrence, Kansas, could have known Hemingway, Mrs. Hinman could have.

Still, those of us who drank at the Gaslight felt a bit sad for her. What must it be like for a woman who once walked up and down *Boulevard Montparnasse* stopping for a champagne cocktail at the Dome or the Select with Jake Barnes or Lady Brett Ashley; a woman who probably bought and borrowed books from Sylvia Beach, but who we could see walking along Jayhawk Boulevard past the Gaslight to stop next door at the Abington Book Shop— not a bad bookstore to be sure, but not Shakespeare and Company. One of us (I won't say who) thought we might invite her in for a red beer; it was not an invitation we would have made to Professor Hinman, but to Mrs. Hinman it seemed possible.

There were twelve of us admitted into the seminar on Shakespeare's tragedies (well, eleven plus one gatecrasher). My colleagues were very serious graduate students, some of them well on their way to Ph.D.s; one had just been signed to a three-year contract to teach at a great East Coast University.

During the semester each of us was to present a seminar paper which was mimeographed (it was that long ago) and handed out the week before so that the following week the author could be questioned ("grilled" was more like it, when it came to the graduate students—but never Professor Hinman). Mine had been on "false hope" in *King Lear*. It was, among all the papers presented, bereft of footnotes. (I didn't quite know how to do footnotes; also, I had contracted a chronic aversion to literary research.) But I wrote well enough to be amusing:

It would be as if a Western Kansas rancher fenced off his High Plains open-range pastures and cut out ten sections to one daughter, ten sections to another, and ten sections to a third. That's a lot of fencing, and even (maybe especially) among siblings, it will most surely make for spite fences and not good neighbors.

Then there was my take on Mrs. Lear: *Where in all this family food fight is Queen Lear? She'd put a stop to it. Just drop dead and leave me the ranch,' you can hear her say to her old fool of a husband. But no. Hers is an entrance blocked by a bear of a bard who doesn't want the trouble. Very convenient.*

"I see there are no footnotes to document these bizarre opinions," the graduate student with the three-year contract said. Professor Hinman smiled.

Among the other un-footnoted bizarre opinions I expressed was that …*what woman in her right mind would want fifty hunters traipsing through her kitchen on opening day of pheasant season—or any day for that matter? When you give up the home place, you'd better buy a ranch house in Kansas City and take up golf. And aren't we being a bit editorial with the name 'Goneril?' We all took Health in high school: Goneril-Gonorrhea. We get it. Clap, clapp, clap.*

At some point I did get around to the thesis of my title: *Abandon Hope All You Who Enter Lear,* with examples: that (Lear hopes) Cordelia will win the flattery contest with her sisters; that Gloucester will smell the moral rot of Edmund; that Kent will (we really hope) bring Lear to his senses; and on and on until the end when there is this from Lear himself: *Lend me a looking glass. / If that her breath will mist or stain the stone, / why then she lives.* All of it quoted, but none of it footnoted, nor cited by act and scene.

When my final draft was returned, Professor Hinman noted (among more than a few corrections in my appalling spelling) that *expectations* might have been a better choice than *hope.* But he also observed that *Abandon Expectations All You Who Enter Lear* did not have quite the right ring. Even then, I understood sly irony, and was flattered.

On my exit through the door of the seminar room the night I read my paper, Professor Hinman's smile turned to a small pat on my back. A man forbidden by his calling to use *ibid* or *ff* was perhaps pleased—or at least amused—at my scholarly irreverence. That's the twist we put to it over beers at the Gaslight late into the night.

"Mr. Day, is it?" Professor Hinman says again looking at my sheet of paper.

"Yes."

"Yours are very curious topics: *But yet...*; *Something* does *come of nothing*; and *There* is *cause in nature that makes these hearts hard.*"

Professor Hinman pauses, then says:

"I think you have it wrong. Not that I don't catch your change of wording from *Is there no...* to *There is....* in order to make a point, but I think it ends with ... *hard hearts?* Not ...*hearts hard.*

I am about to ask Professor Hinman if he had caught my mistake (which I had not) because of his training as a Textual Scholar, when the phone on the table behind him rings. He looks at it as if it is a contrivance designed to interrupt his concentration.

"Hello, Charlton Hinman. How may I help you? ... No, it is not too early here. You have reached me at my office. ... In Kansas. At the University. ... Yes, I suppose it must seem very remote. I am a professor here. In fact I am just now meeting with a student. No, not Virginia. Kansas.

It turns out that on the other end of the line is an editor for *The Times Literary Supplement* in London. At the Gaslight Tavern we would mock those students at Harvard or Yale or John(s) Hopkins or the University of Virginia for knowing less than we did, because we knew they existed while they did not know about us. Later this afternoon I will expand that jest to London, but not *The Times Literary Supplement,* about which we did not know. Nor had it occurred to us the importance of 1964 in the world of Elizabethan letters.

"That is very kind of you," says Professor Hinman.

He looks out the window onto the lawn while listening (I suppose) more intently to the voice from London. It was a very long distance for a call to travel in those days.

"Again, you are very kind to say so, but I am afraid I must decline. I want to make some corrections to a recently published book of mine for a possible second edition. But more important, I am this spring teaching a number of good students who deserve my attention. Then there are exams to read the end of the month …No. Not in Maryland. In Kansas. Yes. We are reading the tragedies. In fact, I have a student in my office now with some curious topics for his final exam."

Professor Hinman smiles at me, then, after a long pause, says:

"Well, again, thank you, but I'm afraid not. Such an 'appreciation,' as you call it, would require…"

Another long pause.

"Alas, I am not the kind who 'dashes things off.' I would be pleased to make a recommendation if you like. Just a moment while I concentrate my thoughts.…

"Yes. You might ask Mr. O. B. Hardison of the Folger Library in Washington or Professor Fredson Bowers at the University of Virginia.… You're very welcome."

Professor Hinman puts down the phone and after a moment says:

"Imagine wanting a "dash-off essay" on the meaning of Shakespeare four hundred years out. And in two weeks. What do you think, Mr. Day?"

Not knowing who had called, I thought I might give it a try since Professor Hinman didn't. Most of my writing for the English Department was dash-off, and usually the night before. With two weeks notice I could read some of the plays and get *Monarch* notes for the rest.

"Imagine," Professor Hinman says again.

"Who wants the essay?" I ask.

"*The Times Literary Supplement* in London," he says. "They seem not to know the location of Kansas. And I suspect they think there are Indians in wigwams on the lawn. How provincial."

He looks at the phone and shakes his head slightly.

"Is it true, sir, that you were a bombardier during the war?" I ask.

Professor Hinman laughs. To this day I remember it as deep, prolonged laugh. He puts his right hand over his mouth and touches the top of his forehead with his fingertips, tapping it. He turns to look at the window at the wigwams on the lawn. At least I had not asked if he had dropped the bomb on Hiroshima.

"Well," he says at last. "I had not heard that one. Very odd these stories that go around the students. I wonder what you say of Jane? Don't tell me. But since you asked, no, I was not a bombardier, but I was in the Navy and knew about the attempt to collate reconnaissance photographs, a technique I thought might work to collate Shakespeare's plays. Do you know about collating, Mr. Day?"

Mr. Day does not.

"Well, if you admire a writer as much as I admire Shakespeare, you want to know what words he used and not what, by a printer's accident, was substituted. It would be later the same problem with Joyce."

"James Joyce?"

I am about to ask Professor Hinman if he had seen Josephine Baker dance when he continues, explaining in some detail how he came to build the Hinman collator (out of scraps of spare parts), how it works (by optical magic), what it does (find words that "jiggle"), and that there is one in the basement of Watson Library, where our seminar meets.

"Maybe I should take our class downstairs to see it one evening," Professor Hinman says, more to himself, I thought, than to me. Then again looking at the lawn outside his window he continues: "We had such a lawn at the University of Virginia, where I was a graduate student. Lovely."

Turning back to me he says:

"We need to talk about your topics, Mr. Day. I am curious about 'But yet…' What do you have in mind?"

"I noticed it twice in *Lear*," I say. "Toward the beginning Cordelia uses it about her father, and later Lear uses it about Cordelia. I can't quote the passages, but I wrote them in my notebook."

"'But yet, alas, stood I within his grace.'" Professor Hinman says.

"Yes," I say.

"And 'But yet thou art my flesh, my blood, my daughter.'"

"Yes."

"Mr. Day, you have committed scholarship."

I was hoping the Falstaffs at the Gaslight wouldn't hold Professor Hinman's observation against me, but I wasn't sure.

"I think 'But yet…' is your best choice," says Professor Hinman, looking again at my list. "Yes, by far the best because it will be the most difficult to expand into a coherent essay, and I take it from your previous work you rather like difficult topics."

He folds my list in half and hands it to me.

"Yes," he says. "'But yet…' Anything else, Mr. Day?"

"It's about footnotes, sir."

"I notice you don't use them," he says.

There is a knock at the door.

"Is it true that textual scholars use only special footnotes?"

I am about to be an exit pursued by a professor's standing up. But before he says "Come in, please," he says, "My colleagues in the English Department tell me you are a writer. What an amusing idea you have about textual scholarship. You must use it in a story sometime. Come in, please."

On my way out I pass the graduate student with the three-year contract who enters with a flourish but seeing me, no smile.

Vladimir Nabokov: 1899–1977

There is a National Education Television film in which Vladimir Nabokov is asked what he thinks of his reading public, and he says that his main audience (his only audience) is himself and Vera, his wife. Then he pauses, and says he is often pleased and amused by the cards and letters he gets from all over the world, from "remote places such as Kansas," and that these readers have sometimes taken from his work the same pleasure he had when he composed it. I like to think Nabokov was speaking of me.

In the early 60s I took off a spring semester from my studies at the University of Kansas in order to "read." That was fashionable in those days, especially if you were a "serious literary student." The idea was that you would read the writers the literary departments at the university were not teaching: B. Traven, J. R. Salamanca, R. S. Thomas, J. F. Powers, Philip Larkin, Amos Tutuola, Chinua Achebe, Frank O'Connor, Brendan Behan, Elizabeth Bowen. And Vladimir Nabokov.

In those days I lived in a farmhouse south of Lawrence, toward Lone Star Lake. The house and farm were owned by the Widow Dunn, a small feisty woman who would stop by every day to "check up on things." (That spring she wondered aloud why I wasn't in school more). The agreement I had with Mrs. Dunn was that I would do a certain amount of work each week in order to pay part of the rent. It was dollar-an-hour work, and most of it was tacking old barbed-wire fence back into very old (and consequently very tough) Osage Orange fence posts. If you were lucky, you could find a split in the wood and start there—unless you were The Widow Dunn, in which case you drove in the staple anywhere without any trouble at all.

I recall all this because that spring when I didn't go to school, I also tried not to work much for Mrs. Dunn, and I took to hiding in a back room, a copy of one of my authors with me, until Mrs. Dunn assumed I wasn't home or was "with someone"—as she once put it.

Reading these writers (I was nineteen at the time) was a little like driving in staples: I did not see the point to it, except to get it done—to be well-read; and it was difficult work. There was, however, a certain pleasure to be taken at finding passages where my efforts paid off—where I understood the pleasure the author was taking in his or her own writing. But on the whole, many of the books I read that spring eluded me, and I recall more clearly J. D. Salinger's *Catcher in the Rye*, and Holden Caulfield's theory of literary criticism: A good book will make you want to call the author. Salinger, it turned out, could not be reached by phone, and it did not occur to me to call Nabokov. Now, when I want to, I can't.

Years later (after I'd read many of his novels and much of his other writing) I was bewildered—and still am—by the criticism that Nabokov was a writer of sheer technique whose final achievement would not include an ability to say anything about the pleasures and pains of being human.

Nabokov is a cold writer, I'd read in the literary journals. He is mostly strategy, I was told by one of my teaching colleagues. He is arch; he is arrogant. He is brutal; he is ascetic. He writes without concern for his characters and moves them around like so many chess pieces—or pins them wriggling to a board like butterflies. His novels burn without warmth. I never thought any of this to be true, and even in my initial difficulty with reading *Pale Fire* and *Lolita* I did not think Nabokov heartless.

Nabokov's affection for technique, for what he called "aesthetic bliss," does not mean he is without insight into human nature. His genius is in his sense of proportions and design, so that what is amusing and what is poignant is tumbled together in a way that reminds us of our own lives. Even now he seems to me a nostalgic writer who used his craft to keep his characters and his books from drifting into sentimentality. In that National Education film, Nabokov talks of the pleasure of writing—a pleasure he says comes from first finding the correct word or phrase or detail—the one that had until its discovery eluded him. Beyond that, there was "…the diabolical thrill of having cheated creation by creating something yourself."

What shows in all of his work is a strong affection for making good sentences, splendid paragraphs, and wonderful descriptions. When, at the end of *Lolita*, Humbert writes: "I am thinking of aurochs and angels, the secret of durable pigments, prophetic sonnets the refuge of art. And this is the only immortality you and I may share, my Lolita." I know that while Humbert is writing about his lover, Nabokov is writing about his book by the same name.

It took me quite a while to read more of his novels and stories, and perhaps I should be glad that I did not get on with him too well that first spring south of Lawrence, the Widow Dunn trying to flush me out for work. The truth is I didn't read another Nabokov book for years. I was teaching in western Kansas and for some reason a publisher sent me a copy of *The Defense*—a story of a gentle and awkward man who plays championship chess, and who falls in love in odd ways—and who dies. It started me up again and soon I was rereading *Pale Fire* and *Lolita*, and later *The Gift*, *Bend Sinister*, *Speak Memory*, *Mary* and *King, Queen, Nave*.

But it was after reading *The Defense* that I wrote to Nabokov to tell him (*a la* Holden Caulfield) that I liked that book among others, and in what ways, noting that Horace had written "there can be no art with out craft." I wrote him in care of his publisher, and I have no idea if he ever got it. There was no reply. But when I saw him peering at me out of that National Education Television film to say that he was amused at the letters he got from such "remote places as Kansas" I thought he must be speaking of me. I wish I'd called.

Well, he is dead now. I think it was Hemingway writing about the death of Conrad who said he was sorry he had read all of Conrad because now there would be nothing new of his to read. I know how Hemingway felt. I have saved back nothing of Nabokov's. It is there to read again, and that will be great pleasure, but it is not the same as having the writer alive and well, and working on something new in his room in Montreux, Switzerland, where, were he able to answer the his phone, I would say: "Your immortality is safe within the refuge of art."

We'll Always Have McSorley's

When I was in college at the University of Kansas in Lawrence, Kansas, my friend Harris and I made "pilgrimages" to towns we'd read about. Or places in songs. One summer we drove my open top CJ-5 ranch Jeep (with the windshield down as we cruised through cities large and small) to Bangor, Maine—all because of Roger Miller's "King of the Road."

On the way we stopped just shy of Bangor at Old Town where we discovered a boat builder. After checking our pocket money and double-checking our bank balances, we bought a canoe and rigged it as a top for the Jeep so that we sailed along in shade. The canoe was red like the Jeep. People would honk and wave and flash their lights.

However, we were not tempted by Glenn Campbell's "Wichita Lineman." Too nearby—especially if you drove the main roads. And there was no *there* on the way to Wichita unless you counted Hutchinson's "world's largest grain elevators"—which we did not. Even if William Inge and William Holden did. And we would have been driving to the wrong Wichita.

But a few years later, after we were both out of graduate school, Harris and I once again headed out (same Jeep; windshield down through Salina, Hays, Atwood, Buffalo Gap; no canoe) for Scarborough Fair (which we thought was in northern California), only to get as far as Deadwood,

South Dakota, and the graves of Bill Hickok and Calamity Jane, where we ran out of money. It was later that we learned our destination was not only in the wrong country, but in the wrong century as well. Ours was a road not possible to be taken.

However, before that misguided adventure, there was the semester Harris and I enrolled in an American literature class taught by a celebrated visiting multi-adjective New York University professor. Just before spring break, he observed that southern novels were "grotesque and gothic"—and as such their details are *exaggerated*: "There is more Spanish moss and kudzu in Capote's fiction than in fact," he said.

Harris and I thought to find out for ourselves so we drove to New Orleans (this time in Harris's Daimler convertible—top down) where we discovered Spanish moss and kudzu in a plentitude that even Capote had not imagined. Plus a streetcar named Desire. And a tavern called Ruby Red's with a lovely Vargas girl framed on the wall behind the bar, and an equally lovely one tending the bar. Peanut shells on the floor. We were two days late getting back to campus. By then our multi-adjective professor had sailed on to Jack London's *Sea Wolf*, where in "*real life*" men were "*not that mean to one another*."

Which brings me to this: one blue-blizzard winter night while studying for an American poetry exam, I discovered the following lines from an e.e. cummings poem the editor of the anthology had titled "Snug and Warm Inside McSorley's": *i was sitting in mcsorley's. outside it was*

New York and beautifully snowing. It seemed like a good place to be with Whittier making *coldness visible* on the vast prairie just outside the frosted window of my barely heated (frugal landlady) garage apartment. Not that I knew where McSorley's was—or what it was. At least it was snug and warm.

"It's a bar," said Lola, my girlfriend in those days. "In New York City." Lola was an art history major. "Somebody from the Armory Show made a painting of it. I'll find it for you."

"Let's go," said Harris. It is a week later. We are at the Gaslight Tavern drinking red beers and looking at an art history book opened to John Sloan's *McSorley's Old Ale House*. "We can leave after Christmas and be back when classes start."

"You want to come along?" I asked Lola.

"If I'm going to make a 'pilgrimage'—as you guys call them—to a bar, I'd rather go to the *Folies Bergère* and have champagne." We didn't know where that was either, but it probably wasn't in Kansas.

"Besides," she said, "I can't get into McSorley's." She put a copy of Joseph Mitchell's *McSorley's Wonderful Saloon* on the table with her art history book and our beers.

"Why not?" Harris asked.

"No women allowed," she said, opening Mitchell's book to the first chapter. "Read it yourself."

"Where'd you get it?" I asked?

"The Abington," she said.

The Abington Bookstore was next to the Gaslight Tavern and sometimes after lunch we'd go over and wish we'd spent less money on tomato beers so we could buy the used books the owner, John Fowler, had for sale. Until he opened his store, the only used books we knew existed were in the library.

"It's autographed," I said, looking at the title page. I had never seen an autographed book before.

"It's your Christmas present," she said. "When you get to McSorley's, write me a letter. I want to know if it's still the way Mitchell describes it. And if it looks like Sloan's painting. Especially if it looks like the painting. I'll write you from Paris."

Harris and I did not go to McSorley's that winter break. But I remember putting Lola on a TWA triple-tailed Constellation to New York with a connecting overnight flight to Paris where she was to begin a semester-abroad program in Art History. It was a blue-cold-blizzard-is-coming kind of prairie day. Not a trace of snugness to be found. She turned at the top of the boarding ramp and waved good-bye.

* * *

In the files of the Detroit Institute of Arts there is the following document:

Department: American Art before 1950.

Title: McSorley's Bar.

Classification: Painting.

Artist: John Sloan, American, 1871-1951.

Birthplace: Lock Haven, Pennsylvania, United States, North America.

Date Label: 1912.

Made/manufactured: New York, New York, United States, North America.

Description: Dark-toned painting of men standing around a bar drinking and talking. In center, a bartender on one side of the bar and a waiter on the other side.

Attributes:

   Medium: canvas.

   Medium: oil.

   Medium: paint.

   Search keyword: GENRE.

Dimensions: 26 x 32 in.

   66.0 x 81.3 cm.

Framed: 32 7/8 x 39 1/4 x 3 in.

Signed: Signed lower right: John Sloan.

Related Works: cf. Brown, M.W., THE STORY OF THE ARMORY SHOW, New York: 1963, p. 291.

Notes: No liquor was ever sold at McSorley's, only ale. List price for the painting was $500 in the 1913 Armory Show catalogue.

* * *

I've lost track of the 1960s. At least its chronology. It's not a matter of *Puff, the Magic Dragon*, but the decade seemed scrambled even as it was happening. No narrative; all abstract montage. Everything used. But not much signed. More than all the flowers gone. In my case: a book, a friend, a girlfriend. I never sent the letter I wrote—but then, neither did she.

It turned out that the summer past the afternoon I had been looking at John Sloan's painting in Gaslight Tavern in Lawrence, Kansas, I am sitting in McSorley's "Wonderful Saloon" on Seventh just off Third Avenue in New York City—not far from Cooper's Union.

It is my first trip to Manhattan and I have already discovered that the A-Train is more than track three on my long playing Columbia Record Club LP; that there is a hospital with the same name as a lip-kissing, candle-burning American poet; that the White Horse Tavern has (not unlike our Gaslight Tavern) a used bookstore close by (more than one); and that Henry James's *Washington Square* is my Washington Square—at least mine because that summer I am living in an apartment facing the east side of it.

The NYU professor had been "impressed" by my essay on *Other Voices, Other Rooms* ("required reading"), and especially impressed that I had compared it (unfavorably) to George Washington Cable's *The Grandissimes* (not even listed as "suggested reading"). During my conference, he wondered if I might be willing to house-sit his apartment during the summer while he went to Italy in search of Edith Wharton's *Roman Fever*.

"It's in the East Village," he said. "Do you know the Village?" A village in a city didn't make sense to me, but I said yes. What did I know? To paraphrase Montaigne ten years before I was to read him.

Starting that June, I will spend three months on Washington Square, taking lunches at McSorley's, watching the NYU students, the Irish cops, and the several cats come and go—all the while using my pocket knife to carve *University of Kansas* into the wooden table by the window on the right as you go in. Two dark ales for a dollar; a liverwurst sandwich with thick-sliced raw onions, rich mustard, salt-less crackers, two dollars. Sure enough, men only.

There were free postcards at the bar that McSorley's would send for you. On the front was a picture of the front door (open) with a bald man sitting with his back to us in a chair on the left-hand side studying (I now imagine) the clientele. Two ale barrels converted to flowerpots flank the door. On the backside across the top is printed (in various typefaces): *McSorley's Old Ale House, 15 East 7th Street, New York City (Bet. Second & Third Aves.) A Landmark of Old New York. Since 1854 this famous Old Ale House has been known for its fine home-cooked food and excellent Ale served to a world-wide male clientele.* Across the bottom was printed: *P.S. Meet me in McSorley's.* It is what I would circle with each postcard I wrote to Harris and Lola.

As it was summer, *outside it was beautifully snowing* would have to wait: the promise I've made to return one winter night to live inside the language of the poem has by now become a mantra: *sitting in the din thinking drinking the ale, which never lets you grow old blinking at the low ceiling.*

At that table by the window with the sunlight coming in off Seventh Street, I'd read and reread Joseph Mitchell's book to find what was in the prose that was still on the walls—and to learn (not that I knew it then) how you write with clarity.

Behind the bar was a large copy of John Sloan's *McSorley's Bar*. The waiters are in white aprons, both in and out of the painting. Men are talking in twos and threes toward the door where I am sitting, reading, eating, and carving. The back room is where Mitchell puts it: (*Old John [McSorley] believed it impossible for men to drink with tranquility in the presence of women; there is a fine back room in the saloon, but for many years a sign was nailed on the street door, saying, NOTICE. NO BACK ROOM IN HERE FOR LADIES.*)

Every now and then I'd look outside onto Seventh Street for Lola. In my mind's eye, she would find me (how or why was never in the plot of the story I was writing in my head), and I would watch her for a moment from inside as she would double-check the address on the postcard, then look up to see if the card's picture matched the front of the bar— ale barrels and all.

I would surprise her by coming out onto the street, where through the open door we'd look at the Sloan, and the cats, and the men leaning their chairs on two legs against the wall. Then we'd walk over to the White Horse, where women were allowed and where I had taught the bartender how to make a red beer. By August I understood how you can have a village in a city.

* * *

That summer I got so I knew the names of the streets around where I lived: Hudson. McDougall, Thompson, Bleecker, and in walking them, made a map of the Village in my mind's eye. Most of the time, I would walk in the mornings when it was cool. In the afternoons, I would either go back to the apartment or find a movie. Once I saw *Picnic*, with Kim Novak trying to get herself out of Hutchinson, Kansas. It was as if I was being followed.

In the evenings I would usually make myself a meal from a deli I liked near Cooper's Union, then go out again, at times stopping by the jazz clubs as the music spilled into the streets. There were days when I would take long walks uptown, and in this way I ran into the environs (I did not know the word then) of Woody Allen's movies that were to come into my life later. And other movies as well—now all famous in my mind: the scenes off Central Park in *Midnight Cowboy*—as well as Ratso and Joe Buck deep in the Bowery below where I was living. And in Arthur Laurent's *The Way We Were*, there is that plea from Barbara Streisand to Robert Redford not to go back to his lover on Beekman Place. By the time I see the movie I have been there before. Over the years, I have had the sense that the city—especially the Village—has been making multiple pilgrimages in my direction. The transmigrations of treks.

Some days I would walk to the West Village and take my lunch at the White Horse Tavern. When I did, I'd lick the thumb of my right hand, punch it into the palm of my left hand, turn my fist around and pound it into the palm on the spot where I had put my thumb. It is what we do in Kansas to seal the good luck you have for seeing a white horse in a pasture as you drive along—say in a red ranch Jeep—canoe or not. If you're with your girlfriend, you get a kiss. Even at the White Horse, I kept looking.

I was trying to be a writer. I had my portable Remington; the professor said I could have the kitchen table as my desk. To warm up, each day I'd type on Lola's letter, using the small sheets of yellow sketchpad paper she had given me. After a paragraph or two, I would put what I had written into Mitchell's *McSorley's* as a bookmark. Then I'd begin my own work—a novel set on the western high plains of Kansas into which I stuffed as many grotesque details (coyote hunters bringing to town bundles of ears, each attached by a strip of skin, to claim the bounty at the county office) and as much profanity ("He's lower than snake shit at the bottom of a post hole.") as the prose could carry in hopes that one day a famous multi-adjective professor would lecture that western Kansas cannot be all that bizarre and profane. He, too, would be wrong.

Neither the novel nor the letter was ever finished.

* * *

In Joseph Mitchell's *McSorley's Wonderful Saloon*, there is this:

At midday McSorley's is crowded. The afternoon is quiet. At six it fills up with men who work in the neighborhood. Most nights there are a few curiosity-seekers in the place. If they behave themselves and don't ask too many questions, they are tolerated. The majority of them have learned about the saloon through John Sloan's paintings. Between 1912 and 1930, Sloan did five paintings, filled with detail, of the saloon—"McSorley's Bar," which shows Bill [McSorley] presiding majestically over the tap and which hangs in the Detroit Institute of Arts;

"McSorley's Back Room," a painting of an old workingman sitting at the window at dusk with his hand in his lap, his pewter mug on the table; "McSorley's at Home," which shows a group of argumentative old-timers around the stove; "McSorley's Cats," in which Bill is preparing to feed his drove of cats; and "McSorley's Saturday Night," which was painted during Prohibition and shows Bill passing out mugs to a crowd of rollicking customers. Every time one of these appears in an exhibition or in a newspaper or magazine, there is a rush of strangers to the saloon.

* * *

In my mind's eye, the Mitchell edition I am reading that summer is a paperback with a thick, perfect, bound spine (a little dry as it finally cracked, and I bound it back together with a pair of rubber bands) that was published—or had something printed on it that made me think it was published—by Universal Books. Is it red? Does it have a big U in its design? Looking at the printing history in my present edition (Pantheon), it might have been published by Duell, Sloan and Pearce. Whenever I am in a used bookstore, I browse the M's. I'll know my book by its spine. Or rubber bands. Or yellow bookmarks.

One night I walked down Thompson Street to the Village Gate at the corner of Bleecker. I had never gone in, but at times during the day when I passed by, I could hear music coming out of a basement apartment just below: sad, soulful music. A man playing his guitar.

The Village Gate was always busy with people going

in and out—people who seemed to be at home there, like Harris and I and Lola were at the Gaslight. I'd stand on the sidewalk and listen to the music, sometimes leaning against a lamppost or a car fender eating the pretzel I'd buy from a vendor I liked on Third Avenue. I wasn't cheap; I was careful.

This one night, a guy about my age came out of the basement apartment below the Village Gate, saw me standing by the door, and said: "Go in. There's a trio singing tonight. Two guys and a blond."

* * *

Over the years, what I have come to like about John Sloan's painting is his use of *chiaroscuro*: the ability he has to make perspective (or depth) from a bit of darkness in the composition, a black figure set in contrast to light from a window in a back room, or the apron of a waiter, or the face of a woman wearing a bow. It is also what I have come to admire about Joseph Mitchell's writing: the singular significance of small details that create a depth. Both are portrait painters. As was e.e. cummings.

Let no art history scholar from my past willfully misunderstand me: I know the *lingua franca* of the Renaissance cannot be transferred intact to the work of an American journalist—even an exceptional one like Joseph Mitchell. But in my mind's eye, I am sitting in McSorley's Old Ale House with both the words of Mitchell and the paintings of Sloan as friends, and I am looking past the coal stove into the back room where I see *an old workingman sitting at the window at dusk with his hand in his lap, his pewter mug on the table.* And he is snug and warm and outside it is New York.

* * *

Then one day I lost it. The book. The letter to Lola.

It was a Sunday when I found it gone. It was not in the apartment. Maybe it would be in McSorley's. Maybe on the bench where I'd sometimes sit in Washington Square and where, after I had paid my way into the Village Gate to hear the blond and two guys sing, I saw the blond reading the paper.

Maybe I'd put it down when I bought my pretzel over on Third Avenue. Or on the counter at the deli near Cooper's Union. But in three days of looking and asking, it was none of those places, and more places than those. Not the White Horse Tavern either, no matter how many times I poked my thumb into the palm of my hand and thumped it while telling the Deity of Lost and Found that I'd trade a kiss for a book. No.

* * *

The ranch where I worked part-time to put myself through school (and later as well) had a large pond on which I had put the canoe. The summer I was in the Village, a tornado came through, and while it did not do much damage to the houses and barns in the ranch yard, it tore up a duck blind we had built on the pond and lifted the canoe and sent it sailing across two sections to the ranch just east of us. There it stayed for a number of years—not found by the rancher (or by us as we didn't think to search that far)—until one summer we lost a few heifers and I drove the Jeep over to look for them in our neighbor's pasture.

Part of the canoe (the stern?) was broken up against the base of an old windmill with bits and pieces in the bottom of the abandoned tank. From there I could see in the pasture other parts (a cane seat, strips of canvas, ribs as if from a dead calf you sometimes find in draws when they've not made it through the winter) all scattered "abouts," and "here-abouts"—as we say in that country. Together you would not have taken it to be a canoe, and maybe that is why our neighbor never called us about it. Besides, how many ranch hands have a canoe?

I write this because before Lola flew off that "coldness visible" day for New York and Paris, I told her I'd take her for a ride in the canoe when she came back. We'd mosey along with me paddling from the stern and she from the bow, not going anywhere but in slow circles, talking around the pond. It would be a fine late summer day. After awhile we'd have lunch on the bank with a bottle of French wine she'd brought back. A prairie boating-party lunch, now that I know what that might look like. Doves in and out of the cottonwoods on the dam. Warm into the night even after the butane light of the ranch yard came on, we'd talk: She would tell me about Paris and the *Folies Bergère*, and I would tell her about New York and McSorley's. And how one day I would show her the Village on our way to her showing me Paris. Stars falling out of the August sky.

* * *

My present *McSorley's Wonderful Saloon* is a used Pantheon hardback edition with a dust jacket photograph of McSorley's in a brown sepia tone on the front. The photograph takes in not only the front of McSorley's (ale barrels, door closed, no snow) but also the tenement above it where the various owners of the saloon have lived. On the back of the dust jacket there is a picture of Joseph Mitchell: bald, chin in the palm of his right hand, wristwatch, no rings, left arm over two thick books, tweed jacket, large eyeglasses: bald. I had never seen a picture of him until this one. He does not look like I thought he would. The book was not autographed.

Inside I found a McSorley's postcard addressed to Capt. E. Moyle, USN, US Naval Hosp, New Port, R.I.

> Dear Capt.
> Next time in NY call me at the News (MU-2-1234) & we'll see a good fite or ballgame with Dr. McCabe—Jimmy Powers.

It was postmarked July 30th, 1948. "Fite or Ballgame" is written above *"P.S. Meet me at McSorley's,"* and "with Dr. McCabe" is written below it.

* * *

I write you now that I could not wait for the canoe ride to tell you about New York and McSorley's, and so in my letter I had written some of what I have written here, and more:

About who else I heard that night at the Village Gate; about how I discovered that Sloan had made a painting called *Yeats at Petitpas,* and how I thought on your way back from Paris I would show you where the painting might have been made and tell you that the Yeats in the painting was not the poet we studied in our English courses, but his father; about going into the New York Public Library, past the lions, to find myself where I would one day find George Peppard and Audrey Hepburn in *Breakfast at Tiffany's* and—now that I think of it—where I did not check to see if that is where I had left your *McSorley's*; about how I walked up Fifth Avenue and then through Central Park looking for Holden Caulfield's ducks and back down the Upper West Side looking for the apartment where Zooey was in the bathtub, and Franny was on the couch with her cat, and Bessie was there, and thereabouts. And how I knew *Franny and Zooey* because I had bought the book that summer and read it in the park on the bench where the blond singer would read the paper on Sunday mornings—and once she was at one end of the bench and I was at the other end. Not all is lost.

But it is also true that in that letter I did not tell you how I drove my Jeep to New York at the start of that summer, nor where I parked it, nor how at the end of the summer I drove it up Park Avenue early one Sunday morning and across the George Washington Bridge and asked the man at the toll booth which was the road to Kansas, and he pointed straight ahead and then put a curve into his arm to the west. But it was what he said about the color of the road at the end of his gesture that made us both laugh.

And you do not know that when I got back to the ranch and went down to the pond to see that the canoe was gone, that our paddles were still there, floating on the water with the cottonwood leaves just then starting to fall. Nor do you know how I learned why Harris did not answer my postcards.

Lola, there is more that I have not written both in your lost letter and in this; there is more I could write here and now: Yes, there is. But instead, how about—absent a canoe ride—we meet one winter day, snug and warm, inside McSorley's, at a table on the right by the window as you go in, you looking up to see if you've got the correct place, maybe holding after all these years, one of the postcards I sent you.

Times have changed: you have been to Paris (and so have I); these days we can both have two dark ales and look at the Sloan behind the bar, the cats, the men leaning their chairs on two legs against the wall, the *chiaroscuro* of the back room. We can order liverwurst and onion sandwiches and talk about what we think has changed in McSorley's from what Joseph Mitchell wrote—and especially from what John Sloan painted. Then I will tell you what has not changed between us. Outside it will be beautifully snowing.

TEACHING

Foreword to TEACHING

In puritan New England in the seventeenth century, there was a custom called "sending out": children routinely were sent away by their families to be raised in other homes. Samuel Sewall of Boston, whose diaries have been invaluable to historians, kept a "sending out" record of his own children. Mary at the age of five was sent to Boston to learn to read and knit; Hannah was almost fourteen when she was sent to Rowley to learn housewifery; Elizabeth, at fourteen years and eight months, was sent to a family in Salem to learn needlework; Joseph was fifteen when he was sent off to Cambridge to attend college. Samuel in 1694 was apprenticed to a Boston artisan; he was sixteen years old.

The historian David Hackett Fischer gives us several reasons for this custom: to prepare children for an occupation, to place them near schools unavailable at home, to avoid local plagues or epidemics, or to put them in intact homes in the event one of the parents had died. It was also assumed that children would learn better manners and behavior in another home and might be protected from certain temptations. "It is certainly more than a coincidence that it was exactly at this age that they all left home to be subjected to outside discipline and freed from the incestuous dangers of crowded living."

For families who could afford it, these purposes were served in later times by boarding schools and military academies. For poor families, there was the alternative of entering the adult world of work, including the military services. In agricultural regions, children could be and were turned into farm laborers at an early age; seven or eight was not too young to become an economic asset. In industrial regions, children were easily trained for factory work and could be housed in company-owned dormitories; forty percent of all the factory workers in New England in 1832 were between the ages of ten and fifteen, and those numbers increased steadily until the enactment of child-labor laws at the start of this [twentieth] century.

Although the purposes of "sending out" have changed significantly, college has become for millions of young Americans a modern version of that old custom. The college or university is no longer expected to act *in loco parentis*, but it is expected to help provide some focus and direction to the lives of our children, some understanding of the world of the past and the present, some understanding of the world that lies ahead. And, most importantly perhaps, college offers a glimpse of who we might be, not in terms of status, income or fame, but in terms of self-realization, in terms of the separate peace we all must make in our encounters with the world outside.

That is what Robert Day is saying in these essays. They are not about guaranteed outcomes or even about intellectual certainties. They are about the unexplored territories of our lives. They are about possibilities.

—Richard Harwood,
Editorial Columnist, *Washington Post*
1925-2001

"We must be taught as if you taught us not,
And things unknown propos'd as things forgot."
— *Alexander Pope*

The ABCs Of Enlightenment

I've been teaching in colleges and universities off and on for about 25 years. That's 25 years of freshmen—students like yourselves, who are even now eyeballing strange new roommates and discovering that clothes don't wash themselves. Most of us who are professors will devote our first class (your first class) this fall to the basics of the course: the killer reading list, the unforgiving deadlines for term papers, what miserable fate awaits you if you miss an exam. That kind of thing.

But I find myself recently tempted to put the lecture on course mechanics aside in favor of a more general task on how to get a generous education—not just from professors and classes, but from the college at large, and for yourself in particular. If I do give that talk to my opening freshman class (and here I recall Oscar Wilde's remark that he could "resist everything except temptation"), it will be from the alphabet of notes below.

Alphabets. In themselves they are interesting. So is college interesting in itself: as in learning for its own sake. You don't need to go to the Career Placement Office your first week on campus. Yes, you'll want a job when you graduate. But you'll need an education first, and the kind of education that awaits you will light up the job search in ways you cannot now imagine. If you think you need to be something by the time you graduate, tell yourself you want to be enlightened. If you don't know what enlightened means (exactly), look it up (do that now to get in practice for those term papers). You might also want to keep the idea of enlightenment (or the eighteenth-century European philosophy of the same name) in mind: It's a good North Star for any student lost in a sea of academic requirements.

In the meantime, did you know that the word "alphabet" is a combination of the first two letters of the Greek alphabet, alpha and beta—thus in Greek, "alphabet" stands for the whole collection of Greek letters, just as our "ABCs" stand for A through Z—not to mention a number of other concepts of completion. Language is lovely. The history of language is inexhaustibly lovely. Trust me. I am your first professor.

Baseball. Once when playing deep in the hole at shortstop, I thought of a metaphor that yoked baseball to life. The line drive that slashed past me in the middle of my epiphany got me benched for three games.

"Jesus-Larry," said the coach when I came off the field at the end of the inning. "You looked like your wheels were nailed to the ground. That cost us two runs. Jesus-Larry."

"I was thinking," I told him, "about how baseball is more like life than basketball or football, because in baseball you don't keep time, and in basketball or football…"

"I don't need this," said the coach, shifting his considerable chaw from one cheek to the other and shaking his head. "I really don't need this. I need a shortstop who can go to his left if I'm going to win the conference."

If you're not a varsity athlete, join the dorm basketball team. Or get up your own softball team. The more line drives that go by the better—as long as your mind is making its way among the curious connections that even errors of omission can illuminate. And if you find yourself playing shortstop one sunny spring day, consider baseball and life. Basketball and life. Buzzers and final outs. Take it from me: college should be like a languid baseball game, not like the NBA Finals. You'll get to that metaphor soon enough.

C. As in the grade: average. Avoid. You're not going to college to be average. At least an F tells you something finite. You failed. Flat F failed.

Speaking of which, I once taught at a college that thought it was poor psychology to give any student an F. We used U instead. U stood for "unsatisfactory." It was printed on a professor's final grade sheets right below the D just where the F should have been. Some nuthouse dean thought it was better to tell a student that he or she was "unsatisfactory" rather than a "failure." Don't go to schools like that. Get As and Bs. Grades are as real as money. Time is knowledge. Knowledge is freedom. After you graduate you'll learn other equations. They are not replacements for these.

Delphi. Go there. Between your sophomore and junior years. The round-trip fare to Athens from New York this spring was a bargain at around $700 on TWA. There are about 600 days between now and late May 2004. If you save about two bucks a day, you'll have airfare and $500 on the ground. Staying in youth hostels and eating goat shish kebab and roasted corn from the street vendors, you can probably get 50 days out of the money. Save an additional buck a day by not drinking that extra beer (or not smoking at all), and you can spend a whole summer in Europe. But go to Greece first. That's where the idea of a liberal arts education flourished.

After you get into Athens, you can catch a public bus to Delphi. You might have to stand for the three-hour trip because they oversell it. Spend at least three days in Delphi before you go back to Athens. Spend a week more in Athens, then start back west (there's some water here you're going to have to cross) toward Italy. Go to Rome. Spend a week or so in Rome but avoid the Spanish Steps, where you'll just run into everybody else from college who went to Europe. Spend your time in the old Jewish ghetto and in Trastevere. From Rome, go north to Florence for a week. Then take a left toward France and after a while (and after St. Paul de Vence) take a right at Avignon and head toward Paris. Spend all of August in Paris with a copy of the *Plan de Paris* in one hand and *A Moveable Feast* in the other. Look for 27 *rue de Fleurus*.

Here it comes. A series of embarrassing questions. Questions whose answers you think everybody who is going off to college knows, but you don't. Like the dates of the Renaissance. The definition of gravity ("what goes up must come down" won't do). What does "medieval" mean? What countries border Greece? Name two living American poets. And one English one. Who was Paris? Who was the oracle of Delphi? And what *is* that body of water between Greece and Italy?

If you think these questions are being asked of you, you're at the wrong end of the question. College is when you start asking them of yourself.

Emulation. I am thinking of E. M. Forster. The Earl of Kent. Dorothy (not Doris) Day. Cyrus Vance. Frederick Douglass. John Sloan. Jane Austen. Mozart. More on this later. Tobias Smolett. Amos Tutuola. (See **Jefferson, Thomas.** Also **Thomas Jefferson.**)

French. Did you pick a college or university that does *not* require a foreign language? Then require it of yourself. Whose education is it, anyway? Besides, how do you expect to spend August in Paris if you don't know *une fleur* from *une mauvaise herbe?* Miss Stein (at *27 rue de Fleurus*) would be disappointed.

Gainsborough, Thomas; Gershwin, Ira; Graham, Martha. (See **Emulation**).

Hours. Because you attend classes only about 15 hours a week, there seems to be more time in college to study than you can now imagine. By the time you become a senior, there will seem to be less time than you need. What happens in between is this: poor students squander their time. (See

Thomas Jefferson.) Good students plan their time and study in a routine fashion. The way to be a good student is to move the eyeballs across the page from left to right many hours every day. And many days a week. And many weeks every semester.

College examinations are "cumulative"—that is, they add up test to test all the way to the final exam. And into advanced courses. Blow off an early week on the French subjunctive and there is hell to pay when you have to read Proust in the original two years later. Blow off double-bonded carbon compounds and you'll never be able to diagram a detergent molecule. Everybody knows this. You know it. (See **Know Yourself.**)

"I don't want to,"** she says. If you're a guy, you might think she means "maybe," and "maybe" means "yes." Even if you're right, you're wrong. There is a sign in the health center here at Washington College that reads: "If it is against her will, it is against the law." It doesn't take enlightenment to understand "no."

Jefferson, Thomas. You probably think of him as the third president of the United States. In truth he was a one-man college of learning. This is where *emulation* comes in. Before I wanted to be shortstop, I wanted to be a professional basketball player for the Boston Celtics. I thought of myself as Bill Russell, in spite of being short, white and pudgy. Such thinking is called either daydreaming or—if you want to do something about it—emulation.

I stopped daydreaming about being Bill Russell a few

years before the line drive that got me benched. It was a few years later that I began working on my imitation of Thomas Jefferson. It's a lifelong task to which I am not equal. When your freshman English teacher asks you for an example of understatement, you may cite the precious sentence.

When I say I want to emulate Thomas Jefferson, or Dorothy Day or Mozart or Madame Curie or Gabriel Garcia Marquez or Akira Kurosawa, it is not that I want to be like them in all regards. I do, however, want to join the pattern of their minds. Or at least I want a life of the mind that will be as natural to me as it seems to me theirs was or is to them.

This studied affection for the life of the mind in others is, I suggest to you, not unlike reading the books you see mentioned in the books you are reading (which is how I came to read Gothic novels via Jane Austen and *Martin Eden* via Vladimir Nabokov) and an excellent eclectic way to find your way toward enlightenment. Trust in the diversity of your studies. You'll put it all together. Even if it takes the rest of your life. Which it should. (See also **Thomas Jefferson.**)

Know Yourself. (See **Delphi.**)

Lessing, Doris; Lee, Robert E.; Lamb, Charles; Lear, Edward; Lucretius. (See **Emulation.**)

Murphy. He was a campus dog of ours who was famous for begging hamburgers at student picnics. We miss him and have always wanted to honor him in print. Such a tribute is called a eulogy. If a eulogy is in the form of a poem, it is called an elegy. Intellectual terminology is useful, but it puts into mind Samuel Beckett's observation that there is more to art than technique, even if technique is all we can talk about. This is probably true of learning as well. May your education be full of Murphys.

Nabokov, Vladimir. American novelist and literature professor who once had something like the following conversation with a student at Cornell University:

"What kind of tree is that?" he asks the student.

"What?"

"What is the name of that tree?" asks Nabokov. "The one outside my window?"

"I don't know," says the student.

"You'll never be a writer," says Nabokov.

I like the story first because I think it's probably apocryphal (they are the best kind), and second because Nabokov—who I happen to think is a very great writer and must have been a very great teacher—is as wrong as he is right in assertion.

What you have to do is leave the professor's office and find out the name of the tree. If you don't do that, you'll not be a writer. Or a botanist. Some combination of the passion of the scientist and the precision of the artist is needed to be a good student. Look up words that you don't know. Be able to name all the shrubs and trees in your college quadrangle. Learning is, among other things, the accumulation of detail. Have you discovered the name of that body of water between Greece and Italy?

Oxford English Dictionary on Historical Principles Founded Mainly on the Materials Collected by the Philological Society. It was the poet W. H. Auden's favorite book. You might get over a fascination for alphabets, but no well-educated person gets over a fascination for dictionaries. Keep one in your dorm room at all times.

Phones, E-Mail. I was taught by a professor born in the nineteenth century. One of his professors had been taught by Henry Wadsworth Longfellow. My professor—a teacher of American literature—held to the old rule that no student was allowed into the classroom after the teacher had entered. If you tried to get into his class after it had started, you found yourself pulling at a door that Professor Nelson (which was his name) held closed from the other side with one hand while making points in the air about Henry Adams with the other.

This was in the early 1960s, when student academic manners (my own included) were pretty appalling because they were nonexistent. If anybody told us the customs of the college, I don't recall it. I do remember there was lore about how long you were to wait for a teacher to show up for class: five minutes for a graduate assistant, ten minutes for an assistant professor, and so on. Some stories held that a full professor was so august you were to sit in the classroom the entire hour.

Customs of course differ, and the teachers at your college or university may have their own views about these matters. In general, however, a bit of formality is better than none. It tends to show some respect—not a bad attitude to adopt toward those who have spent the better part of their lives studying in order to teach you. Don't wear your hat in the classroom, even backward. And don't call your teachers by their first names unless invited to—even if you hear other students do it.

College is also the time to learn the social grace of talking less on the phone and via e-mail and more in person. I want to see students in my book-filled office, where I feel comfortable. Questions about the nature of an assignment often lead to discussions about the topic at hand. I like students. I like to have my mind triggered by them. I like to lend them books when I realize in my talking with them that Edith Wharton can teach them about the social customs of New York in the nineteenth century better than I can. I am pleased to be respected for my dedication to my profession. Good manners do that.

Question. Of course. And often.

Reed, John; Rhys, Jean; Rousseau, Jean Jacques; Russell, Bill. (See **Emulation.**)

Strunk and White. The *Elements of Style* by William Strunk Jr. with Revision, an Introduction, and a Chapter on Writing by E. B. White. Third Edition. Macmillan Publishing Co., Inc. New York, London. $5.95.

Remember those questions back in Delphi? Let's raise some more: if the play *lays* an egg, does the playwright go home and lie down or *lay* down? When can you use "and/or"?

Would you write: "I think Horace admires Jessica more than I"? How do you feel about the word "finalize"? Would you write "None of us *is* perfect"? Or "None of us *are* perfect"?

True, it's not the final test of being educated, and to be sure your parents might well hope that they don't have to pay piles of college tuition for you to know the difference between *infer* and *imply*. They reasonably hope you got that part of your education in high school. But we know you didn't. Or that it was a wobbly learning at best, and that you cover your tracks by steering clear of *lay* and *lie*, not to mention *me* and *I*.

There are two ways to learn that *it's* is not the same as *its*. The first is the way I learned it. My freshman English teacher at the University of Kansas told us there were four mistakes in writing we could not make or we would get an F at the point of the foul. *It's* for *its* was one of them. You guessed it: Two blue books into the semester I found a great red circle around the *its* of "Its not difficult to describe the relationship between the narrator of the *The Great Gatsby* and Jay Gatsby." My professor's margin note read "I have stopped reading."

The other way to learn all this is to buy the book that heads this section. And read it.

Thomas Jefferson. (See also **Jefferson, Thomas.**) "Determine never to be idle. No person will have occasion to complain of want of time, who never loses any. It is a wonderful thing how much may be done if we are always doing."—Thomas Jefferson to his children.

Unnecessary drinking. College and boozing are an old tradition. Bacchus was probably the president of a fraternity. Times change. Colleges are changing. I know many students who don't drink, and I know many others who won't ride in a car with a drunk as a driver. The former choice is a matter of personal preference; the second is conclusive evidence of sanity.

But truth be told, most of you will drink when you get to college. If that's going to be the case, now is the time to pass this article on to your parents with the paragraphs that follow this boxed off.

There was a story where I went to school about the western Kansas rancher who was about to send his son to the university. In the spring before the boy was to attend, the father visited the campus in Lawrence and went to all the student cafés and beer joints. Some were populated by fraternity types, others had jocks of one kind or another, some were just dives. A few were hangouts for "majors": The philosophy majors tended to gather at the Rock Chalk; the drama majors (the future great actor Moses Gunn among them) gathered at the Jayhawk. And so on.

It became campus lore that the rancher told his son that he would pay the boy's café bill at certain taverns, but not at others. If the young man wanted dinner and a few beers with Moses Gunn, consider it on Dad. If he just wanted to get wasted, consider it just that. I like this story. I know it is true.

Voluntary. Somewhere I read a definition of a student as a person in zealous and *voluntary* pursuit of knowledge.

Alphabets. Enlightenment. Three dollars a day for two years to get to Delphi. Your own list of intellectual heroes. Strunk and White. Your own line drives. All voluntary.

Why? Almost always a good question.

X-ing. "X is a letter, which, though found in Saxon words, begins no word in the English language." So writes Samuel Johnson in his 1755 *A Dictionary of the English Language.* It is his only entry for X. My guess is that his editor was pounding on his door for copy, and although Johnson was learned enough to write a small history of X from the Greeks through Christ, he had to cut it short.

My favorite example of a word beginning with X is *The Oxford English Dictionary's* citation from Edgar Allen Poe's *Tales* (1849): "I shell have to x this ere paragrab, said he to himself as he read it over… So x it he did, unflinchingly, and to press it went x-ed."

This sounds like the old adage that writing is rewriting. But there is something else you'll learn if you prowl out of the OED's X and into Poe's *Tales* to read the story in question ("X-ing a Paragrab"). X is not what it seems to be.

You. (See **Zeal.**)

Zeal. Somewhere I read a definition of a student as a person in *zealous* and voluntary pursuit of knowledge. That's you.

Tales Out Of School

Pressroom, The Rose O'Neill Literary House, Washington College, Chestertown, Maryland, Spring 1991

Mainly they think about sex," says Mike Kaylor, the master printer for the Literary House Press at Washington College and a substitute teacher in various nearby public schools. It is getting late on the Thursday evening of President George H. W. Bush's education speech. Mike and I are printing a run of hand-set posters for the college and talking about teaching. Bad-mouthing, really. Pissing and moaning. Between us we have forty years or so in the classroom, most of them mine. I've been a swimming teacher, baseball coach and Poet in the Schools (by way of a program run by the beleaguered National Endowment for the Arts), but mainly I've taught in colleges and universities for the past twenty-five years: Iowa Writers' Workshop, the University of Kansas, St. Nevertheless-of-the-Prairie (a generic name some of us in the profession give to the kind of colleges that have vice presidents of office-space allotment and offer advanced courses in alligator-farm management). In the lexicon of the faculty lounge, I am bituminous coal. Full of the sulfur of derision and irony. I probably need an industrial scrubber, I am so polluted by the system. I am not yet fifty.

"They think about sex seven seconds out of every ten," says Mike. He has had a bad day. Middle school. At that age students are fuel pumps for hormones. The central administration had called Mike at seven. The regular teacher was out with the kind of student-sponsored virus you're supposed to ship to the Centers for Disease Control in Atlanta. Public school classrooms are like petri dishes, complete with pulled shades to block the sunlight and an overactive boiler controlled by either a consulting firm in Dallas or a secretary in the main office with an out-of-whack thyroid.

"So my problem," Mike continues as he locks up our type, "is that with only three seconds in ten to get their attention, how do I teach the Fourteenth Amendment, much less the Bill of Rights?" "You don't," I say, "Leave the Bill of Rights to Philip Morris. Or Milli Vanilli—whoever he is." I have this firm belief that at any school in the nation you could get more students to attend an event in which Oprah Winfrey stands on stage and either eats or does not eat (whichever she is doing these days) than you could get for a lecture by Cyrus Vance on his principled resignation as secretary of state. It wouldn't even be close, you'll have to admit. "The problem is especially difficult," Mike says, "when you consider that the three seconds they are not thinking about sex are not the same three seconds for each student."

"No doubt," I say. I am trying to remember what it was like to think about sex seven seconds out of ten, and in that way to remember what it was like to be a student: trying—now that I think of it—to remember how I learned when I was the age of Mike's students, and what I learned. The periodic table comes to mind. The states and their capitals—

or was that review from a previous year? Who imports which minerals to us so we can make which products? It seems to me a refrigerator pretty much came from America, but a pencil pretty much came from other countries. And fruit, now that I'm on a roll, came in abundance from the United Fruit Country—a place I could never find on any maps and only later learned was not a country but a company that owned a country. Don't start thinking about exactly what you learned in school or it will depress you greatly.

"I wonder if you could calculate," Mike says, "what the odds would be for every student in my civics class having their three sex-free seconds at the same time."

"A sort of coming together," I say.

"It might make an interesting life-study problem for math," he says. "That's what they have in grade schools these days: 'life-study' problems."

"In colleges, we have the literature of the previous five minutes," I say.

"That's what I hear," he says.

I start to ink the rollers for the press. Red. Deep red. From the O'Neill Literary House kitchen not far from where we are working comes the sound of a coffeepot finishing its run. We are getting into finals and senior-thesis time at the college, and the students who study at the Literary House tend to make their coffee thicker the later in the year it gets. By early May, it has the quality of West Texas crude. When I passed through the readers' room earlier in the evening, there was a heated student debate going on about the wisdom of NOW's President Molly Yard, a recent campus visitor. I could tell it was a diversion, albeit a serious one. In my day, we debated the politics of the Kingston Trio ("They're rioting in Africa, there's strife in Iran"). But sooner or later, I figured, these kids were going to have to drop Molly Yard and face the *Critique of Pure Reason,* if not the sensibility of Jane Austen. The sputtering of the coffeepot is probably a signal they have come to that conclusion themselves.

"If they call me tomorrow for the same class," Mike says as he watches me spin out the ink, "I'm going to teach nothing but the First Amendment. I figure there are about 20,000 seconds in a teaching day, which gives me close to 3,000 seconds for free speech."

"What about food?" I ask.

"I bring my own," he says. "I'd weigh a type case if I didn't."

"I mean when they are not thinking about sex, they are probably thinking about food. You'll have to slip free speech in there between a hot dog and French fries."

"Let's call it a thousand seconds," Mike says. "I think I can get some retention in a thousand seconds. 'Congress shall make no law…'" He is not kidding. Sometimes I think our entire educational system is carried on the backs of teachers like Mike.

"You ready?" I say, looking at the press.

"'Print it as it stands: beautifully,'" he says. The quotation is from Henry James, and it is the motto of our pressroom.

I crank the old Vandercook and lay my hand over the sheet of paper as it rolls onto the bed of type and a linoleum cut of the Literary House that will be our souvenir poster.

Printing teaches you that patience is too ample and simple a pleasure to be called a virtue. It is what I do—what both Mike and I do—when the end of the term seems too full of considerations.

Mike pulls off the sheet and, holding it by the corners like a piece of newly washed laundry, lets it unfurl for me to see: It is the spacious old house where we are working, rendered by Becca Hutchinson, one of the students in the Art Department. There is the large porch that wraps around the front; there is the deck on which the students hold their "Writers' Theatre" productions; there are the open windows of the Mary Wood Readers' Room, where Kant and Jane Austen have won out over Molly Yard; and behind that, the kitchen with its coffee about to solidify.

"Look," says Mike, flipping a free thumb toward the middle of the house. It is my office (stacked in my mind's eye with blue books and term papers), and above that on the third floor are the fellowship rooms where (I hope) one student is typing her Toni Morrison thesis and another is finishing his senior novel. Back down on the ground and toward the rear is the pressroom itself, stocky and red and filled to the brim with type cases, presses, flat files, cartons of paper—and two overweight middle-aged teachers looking at the house in which they are printing a vision of where they work.

"'First, to find out a spacious house,'" I say. It is from Milton's "On Education," and it has risen to the top of my brain again after all these years. Below Becca's engraving, Mike has set a few lines of poetry by the great writer-teacher William Stafford:

Suddenly in this doorway where I stand in this house I see this place again this time the night as quiet, the house as well secured, all breath but mine borne gently on the air.

"What do you think?" Mike says.

The blinding good work before us by people who have been students and teachers, and who have been our students and teachers, gives us—two full-time practicing cynics—pause: Is something going right here?

Despite cultural illiteracy. Despite a would-be "education president" who chose Dan Quayle as vice president. Despite Political Correctness. Despite guns in high-school hall lockers. Despite schools of education and their mistress, Methods Galore. Despite ivy-covered tenure and private-college tuitions that for four years could run to the cost of a Mercedes turbo diesel. Despite the senior art student who once asked a colleague of mine how to mix red. Despite Stanford's yacht and the private planes of the state universities in this country. Despite bituminous-coal me and 1,000-seconds-for-the-First-Amendment Mike. Despite it all, is there accomplishment and education and enlightenment drying on the paper before us deep inside the nineteenth-century printing room of an eighteenth-century college here in the final throes of the twentieth century?

In this season of graduations, I'm thinking, as the voice of the commencement speaker is once again heard in the land, we'd better hope something has gone right with the billions of dollars and seconds per year we devote to education. I look at Bill Stafford's poem and I think back, not only to sex-filled seconds, but to how I learned (from Bill Stafford, among others) and to how I've taught all these years and what my students might have learned. As the scenes come back to me, I think about——dare we mention it in this era?—what it all means. And finally, I wonder if what I know about education, and how I've taught and learned, spells hope or despair for our country. My private heresy is that I think good education is a student moved to emulation. There are days when I'm worth being emulated, and there are other days (I now recall with chills) when I'm not.

The Iowa Writers Workshop, Iowa City, Iowa, 1981

There is a student in my office and one waiting in the hall. The one waiting in the hall is Bob Shacochis, who will become— as author of *Easy in the Islands* and *The Next New World*— one of the fine fiction writers we now have in America. This day he has just sold the story over which we are to have a conference to either *The Paris Review* or *Harpers*. I don't remember which, but I do remember that I did not know about the sale, and so I am soon to make a considerable fool of myself by telling Bob the story is barely readable (much less salable) and that it must be rewritten in about 6,000 ways out of 7,000 words. Remember, the University of Iowa—not to mention the corn farmers of Iowa (not to mention Bob Shacochis)—is paying me good money for this sage advice.

But before I cut loose my considerable critical ability on Mr. Shacochis, I first must confer with a Miss H (I've forgotten her name; you'll soon see why).

Me: "How can I help you?"

Miss H: "I want to be a poet."

Me: "I teach fiction writing. See Mr. Bell. He teaches poetry. He's a poet. A very good poet."

Miss H: "I don't want to talk to a poet. I don't want to be influenced by poets."

Me: "But of course you are influenced by poets when you read poetry. Who is your favorite poet?"

Miss H: "I don't have a favorite poet. I don't read poetry. I want to be a 'unique' poet."

Me (to myself): "My God."

Miss H: "Do you want to read my poetry?"

Me: "No."

Miss H (fumbling in a handbag roughly the size of a hot-air balloon gondola for what appears to be the complete works of Gibbon bound in blue spiral notebooks): "Here. Read one. Please. Read the first one."

Me (in a moment of madness, reading aloud a poem titled "Ryukyu"): "I am nothing / but that which is nothingness itself / sailing like a deep sadness / upon the seas of hopeful longing / looking for an island of bliss / with trees of quiet / and globes of ruthenium."

Miss H: "What do you think?"

Me: "What's ruthenium?"

Miss H: "A rare element found only in Russia. In the poem it stands for the unity of the communist and capitalist systems. I see them coming together on the islands of Ryukyu."

Me (to myself): "My God. Dear God-of-the-Great-American-Novel, keep me from asking about the islands of

Ryukyu; also, 0 Lord, instruct me about how I can get out of this one, and I promise you I'll never teach again."

Miss H: "What do you think of the meaning?"

Me: "Of the poem?" (I am stalling, waiting for a sign.)

Miss H: "Yes. The poem. What do you think of its meaning?"

Me: (sensing myself transformed into an airport guru, complete with white robes and windrow of red hair parting my bald scalp) "I think your poem is both curious and promising. There are words here arranged in lines, and that is neither a bad nor a good thing. The poem is like itself: ruthenium and Ryukyu. Rare and far away. Go now. Write more poems. But show them to no one—not even to me—lest I steal the purity of your vision. Be unique and stay by yourself. Very much by yourself."

All gods work in strange and mysterious ways. Miss H's eyes glaze over in joy. She puts ruthenium and "Ryukyu" back in her balloon bag and leaves my office never to be seen by me again. As far as I know, she is writing poetry in a grass hut east of Taiwan. However, just thinking about the incident has so unnerved me I no longer have the strength to reveal just how badly I advised Bob Shacochis. I assure you, your imagination cannot do justice to the scene.

West Fork, Arkansas, November 1969

I am substituting in the fifth grade. We are reading aloud, one child after another: down one row, up the other. It is the way I was taught to read by Mrs. Browne (I think there was an "e" on it) at Hickory Grove School in Mission, Kansas. You'd read along with the other kids, and when Mrs. Browne got two or three readers away from you, you'd skip down and practice in your mind the passage you figured would be yours. If nothing else, it taught you to pay attention and plan ahead. It probably taught me more than I know:

"Within a short walk of Longbourn lived a family with whom the Bennets were particularly intimate."

If you didn't know a word, you were supposed to say so. In those days there were no glossaries in the books we read, and so it fell to Mrs. Browne—who always seemed to know not only the meanings and pronunciation of words, but when (by some thinness of your voice) you didn't know what you were saying—to instruct you in your language.

"Do you know what 'intimate' means?"

"Yes, Mrs. Browne."

"What?"

"I don't know for sure."

"It means to be very close with people, doesn't it? To have them as your good friends."

"Yes, Mrs. Browne."

When it came your turn—or at least when it came my turn—the reading aloud itself seemed familiar, almost intimate. It is true that in my case I developed an excessive affection for the sound of my own voice, which would sometimes compel me to read beyond the territory of the sentences and paragraphs given to me as my own and into the province of Nancy Fulton, a soft doll of a girl who sat behind me in those days and who lived in a pale yellow house on my way home—at least on a plausible way home:

"The ladies of Longbourn soon waited on those of Netherfield," I read on. And on.

"That will be enough, Bobby," Mrs. Browne would have to say. "It is Nancy's turn."

"Yes, Mrs. Browne."

You always answered Mrs. Browne politely. You could not just say "okay." When you were spoken to, you responded in complete sentences that contained no slang. It was called politeness.

"Nancy, start with 'The ladies of Longbourn…'"

"Yes, Mrs. Browne."

In 1969 in West Fork, Arkansas, matters seem not to have changed that much since my days in the same grade. The children seem to me (this is my first time as a substitute teacher—indeed my first time in the public schools since I went away to college) to have that same mix of respect and friendliness that we had toward Mrs. Browne at Hickory Grove.

The West Fork school has wide, short hallways with maps and clippings about current events tacked to the bulletin boards: We are about to go to the moon these days in West Fork. There are lockers without locks (does that seem possible? Maybe my memory on this point is faulty), and there is even a woman from the cafeteria who comes around and collects lunch money.

"Johnny Legg won't have his," she says as she hands me a tally sheet.

"What do we do?"

"Take fifty cents out of the cigar box in the bottom drawer."

"Shall I put in an IOU?"

"Don't bother."

"I see."

"Chicken potpie for lunch," the woman says to the children as she leaves the room with a wave.

Yay, yay! Says everybody. There is no irony here in West Fork; the children think chicken potpie is going to be a very good thing—and, as I learn at lunch, it is; homemade in a sturdy kind of way with something other than microwave glue for its innards.

In the West Fork classroom itself—and here my memory I know is true—there is no office-to-room intercom; ergo there are no "morning announcements"; no "Mr. Day, send Fred Whitehead to the office"; no "The cheerleading squad will be dismissed from classes today at one-thirty to go to a statewide workshop." The school board of West Fork cannot yet afford the electronics that are teaching most of America's youth it is perfectly fine to interrupt those important conversations we call teaching.

If all this is to the good, what is about to happen is to the bad: It has to do with the story we are about to read, a tale called "Mr. and Mrs. King Triumph Over the Savages." There is, I notice, a small asterisk by the word "savage," indicating that the word will be defined in the back of the book. In this case the definition—which we all look up, and which I read aloud—goes something like: *American Plains Indians of the nineteenth and early twentieth centuries.* So much for subtlety. Not to mention Mrs. Browne's mind as a house of knowledge.

The tale itself is a pitiful account of how the Kings defend their home against American Indians who just won't leave Manifest Destiny alone. While my students dutifully read, I lope ahead to see how it all turns out. What I notice is not so much that it turns out badly for the Indians (it does, of course) but how little the language counts for anything. This—I will later learn—is what state departments of education are calling "adolescent literature."

"Stop," I yell.

Everybody stops. The boy who has been reading stops reading. Everybody else stops breathing. I get up and go toward the back of the room, where I see a closet door. In my mind's eye, it is the door to the book closet in Mrs. Browne's room in Hickory Grove. When I open it, I will find the back and the sides lined with books: *Tom Sawyer, The Sea Wolf, A Tale of Two Cities, Pride and Prejudice.* I open the door in West Fork, Arkansas, 1969. There is an overhead projector, boxes of transparencies and a rubber-banded bundle of grease pencils. On the door I notice a schedule of workshops: This very day West Fork has sent the teacher for whom I am substituting to Fayetteville to study "The Overhead Projector and Modules." It is, I think, the same kind of moment in history as when the Romans installed lead pipes to bring water into their homes.

My Office, Second Floor, The Rose O'Neill Literary House, September 1990

The student in my office wants to be a writer. That's a problem. He already is a writer. A good writer. With a fine sense of invention and a talent for ripping off every other good writer from Chaucer to Calvino. He wants me to be his teacher. He might be better than I am. What I have to do is figure out how to let him learn. This is no easy task. For good students like this young man, you have to create what Henry Adams called an "atmosphere" for learning. Think about it. Who was your best teacher? You, right? Who taught you to be your best teacher? Your second-best teacher, right? Was any teacher so bad as to ruin a good book? (Well, maybe—but he moved on to become superintendent of curriculum.)

"Writers are readers moved to emulation," I say. "Saul Bellow."

"I've never read Saul Bellow," he says. "Would you recommend a book?"

"Try *Henderson the Rain King,*" I say. It is my job to keep the circle of the lamplight friendly for this young writer. I also have a plethora of literary prescriptions I pass out when required. Need a bathroom scene? Try Salinger's "Zooey." Want to know how to write about children? Read Bowen's *The Death of the Heart.* Too many characters on stage? There is always "Exit: pursued by a bear" (Shakespeare). Or: "He went to the province of Y and died of the nameless dread." (Tolstoy, I think). Want to drag somebody behind a ship to attract sharks? Perhaps a bit specialized, I agree, but read *The Sea Wolf*

The young man looks behind me at the row of bookcases. His eyes are so good he can probably read the spines from where he sits: Yukio Mishima, Don DeLillo, Flannery O'Connor, B. Traven. Does he want such authors of his own to one day loom in cases all around him as if they can protect him against mortality? Is that what I am teaching him? If it turns out he loves his learning because of what he sees in my bookcases, am I going to take some credit? You bet I am.

"Write," I say. "Read and write. Bring me what you write and I will read it, and we will talk and see how what you have written is what you want to write and how it is not."

He smiles; he knows.

"May I borrow a book?" he says. Of course.

Pressroom, The Rose O'Neill Literary House, Washington College, Spring 1991

Before we start to crank off more posters, I go out and get two cups of the students' idea of coffee. At our age, one cup will keep us awake until retirement. Mike lights a pipe and fishes in his billfold for a photocopy he found in the middle-school faculty lounge that morning. It reads:

Then Jesus took his disciples up the mountain, and gathering them around him, he taught them saying:

"Blessed are the poor in spirit, for theirs is the kingdom of heaven.

"Blessed are those who mourn....

"Blessed are the meek. ...

"Blessed are the merciful. ...

"Blessed are the peacemakers....

"Blessed are those who are persecuted for righteousness' sake....

"Blessed are you when men revile you and persecute you and utter all kinds of evil against you....

"Rejoice and be glad, for your reward will be great in heaven...."

Then Simon Peter said ...

Do we have to write this down?

And Andrew said ...

Are we supposed to know this?

And James said ...

Will we have a test on this?

And Philip said ...

I don't have any paper.

And Bartholomew said ...

Do we have to turn this in?

And John said ...

The other disciples didn't have to learn this.

And Matthew said ...

Can I go to the boys' room?

And Judas said ...

What does this have to do with real life?

Then one of the Pharisees who was present asked to see Jesus's lesson plan and inquired of Jesus ...

Where is your anticipatory set and your objectives in the cognitive domain?

And Jesus wept.

We don't talk as we take our break.

St. Nevertheless-Of-The-Prairie, Late Spring 1965

I am sitting in the office of the president of the college, a man who, I have been told, has a doctorate of education—in sports administration. I do not believe this. I am very young; it is my first college teaching job. The Department of English has said I should be hired; the dean is out of town for an Elks Club convention.

"What methods do you plan to use in teaching?" says the president.

"Discussion," I say, "and lecture when I want to deliver a lot of information." In truth I am faking it. I have never taught before. Outside on the campus sidewalks I can see students coming and going. It is May; the cottonwood seeds are scattering, and the air is filled with them. I find myself thinking what it will be like. How well will I do? How well do I know my subject?

"There are more than two methods of instruction," says the president. He seems to want an answer.

"I only know discussion and lecture," I say. I have not yet learned to lie to deans and presidents.

"Dr. X"—here he cites an educational authority of whom I have never heard—"lists fifty-four distinct methods of instruction."

This does not seem possible to me. I don't know very much in my early twenties, but I rattle around in my head to see if there can be any better way to learn than to have someone tell you what "intimate" means, or talk it out with someone until you discover what "intimate" means.

"I only know two," I say again. I don't really need this job, I think. I have a job as a small-gasoline-engine repairman at Wilson's Supply for a buck an hour.

"What about books?" says the president, settling back in his chair. I take it that if I can say books are Method No. 26, I have the job.

"Lecture," I say. I see myself bending over a pitted carburetor.

"Filmstrip?" he fires back. "With questions afterwards?"

"Lecture, then discussion." Where is Socrates when I need him?

"What about"—and here I can tell he thinks he has me—"a filmstrip on the discussion method of teaching?" The president of a college in the United States of America actually says this to me. It gets worse. In my memory, I hear the rest of the interview through the kind of hiss that comes over the phone wires to Henry Fonda at the end of *Fail-Safe:*

"They tell me you want to be a writer," says the president, looking at my credentials.

"Yes," I say.

"Do you write letters to the paper?"

"What paper?"

"Any paper. Do you write letters to newspapers causing trouble?"

"I haven't written any letters to any newspapers," I say.

"Well, don't start here," the president says. "I know the editor in town, and he'll just bring them to me and I'll toss them in the trash. And that will be that."

My God, what does it say about me that I took the job?

Pressroom, The Rose O'Neill Literary House, Washington College, Spring 1991

We have started up again and are near the end of our run. A hundred copies. We're going to send some to Bill Stafford to sign. The others we're going to give away. High on caffeine and flushed with the Beatitudes, we have returned to pissing and moaning.

"I know a guy in New York," says Mike, "who wears a different costume every day to teach. He started this about five years ago when he didn't think he could keep going any longer. One day, he's a cowboy with boots and a hat; the next day, he's a doctor with a lab coat. The only one they won't let him wear is the wig when he's a woman. You'd think New York would be more liberal than that."

"One day," I say, "I asked my incoming students if they knew any living American writer. They came up with Thomas Hardy and Barry Switzer."

"Who's Barry Switzer?"

"You don't want to know," I say.

I crank off the last poster and find myself thinking about the blue books in my office upstairs. I had my students take a walk through Chestertown, and for the exam, they were to narrate our journey in the style of one of the authors we have been reading: J. P. Donleavy, Muriel Spark, Elizabeth Bowen, Raymond Carver. During the week, I have been reading their exams and have been stunned by what they know, and the ease with which they know it. It is as if they have learned without effort, learned beyond what I could teach them.

Is this good? In literature we can have *dramatic irony*. The readers know more than the characters do. So if I know my students have learned more than they think, should I tell them? Or can their splendid accomplishment alone make a rough-cut diamond of old coal? I think so.

"I have a teacher friend," says Mike as he numbers the final print, "who went to New Orleans for spring break, where he saw a sign that said: 'Consultant: Divorce, Plumbing, Roof Repairs, Tax Problems. Former Teacher.'"

"How'd it make him feel?"

"Like he had a future."

"It still looks good, doesn't it?" I say as I look again at the spacious house we've made.

"Some days are diamond," says Mike.

Famous Education

Every spring, the college where I teach (Washington College in Chestertown, Maryland) gets an unusual amount of national-press attention for awarding to a graduating senior roughly thirty thousand dollars (circa 1975). That's $30,000. One prize. One senior. What for? For promise in "literary endeavor."

We have awarded it yearly since 1968. It is the Sophie Kerr Prize, so named because Sophie Kerr Underwood of *Saturday Evening Post* fame left Washington College over half a million dollars, half the income to be used to fund the largest undergraduate literary prize in the nation (and one of the largest literary prizes in the world).

Only half the income? That means the other half goes somewhere else, which means the largest undergraduate prize in the nation is only half the story. And the wrong story. At least as far as I'm concerned. I am a writer teaching at Washington College. I am not famous. I fear for my students.

"Have any of the winners become famous?" a reporter once asked me. She was looking at the list of previous recipients; she did not recognize any of the names. General recognition used to be the most obvious qualification for fame.

"One made *People*," I said. "Or *Us* or *We*, I forget. Is that fame?"

"People, yes," she said, "but not *Us."* She made a note to check on it. "All of us will be famous for fifteen minutes," she said.

"Andy Warhol," I said.

"Yes," she said. "What do you think it means that none of the winners have become famous?" she continued. I said I thought God was on their side.

One year, a national evening-news television crew arrived. My college tries to keep the winner secret, but that year, we had to tell the television people, so they could point the cameras in the right direction to catch *(a la* "The Price is Right") screams, gasps, jumping up and down, whoopie, whatever. As it turned out, we did not make the evening news. The woman who won was not animated enough for the camera. For my part, when they pointed the camera my way, I said the prize was larger than my salary that year. I was quite animated.

What madness is this? We are, after all, the tenth oldest college in America and we give a generous education; we are not (largest undergraduate literary prize notwithstanding) in the business of making our students famous. If anything, we are to do something quite the opposite. That's where the rest of the money (and the rest of the story) comes in. And it has nothing to do with fame.

The real prize is the ignored, half-forgotten, generally taken-for-granted thirty thousand dollars that, as one reporter noted, "does not go to the Prize." Where does it go? How is it used? Why is it not famous? What is the nonsense about fame anyway? And to what extent has our national obsession with "winning" produced a game-show mentality among our students? Washington College is not in the literary lottery business. I repeat myself: What madness is it?

The dull answer to the first question is that much of the "other thirty thousand dollars" goes to scholarships, books, funds for student magazines (students published seven little literary magazines at Washington College during the previous year). Our students are famous among the printing press, the typewriters, the mimeograph machines.

The funds are used as well to bring scholars and writers to our campus. Not much fame or news there. No matter how hard we try. And at times we've tried pretty hard. Allen Ginsberg and Peter Orlovsky came to our quiet campus in our placid, rural Eastern Shore town. They walked through the campus, chanting. They tried to levitate our administration building. But our administration building is—like all academic administration buildings—very heavy in spirit and cannot be lifted by mere Far Eastern chanting, much less old Joan Baez folk songs. But it was great fun, and our students (850 non-famous, non-winners of the Prize) learned something about the freedom of what used to be called "non-conformity" and the beauty of the iron line of American poetry.

Once we invited Katherine Anne Porter. She was splendid. Very old and very wise. I remember she spoke too softly for the microphone to amplify her voice (does that seem possible?), and so we all had to gather around her and listen to what she had to say in her non-electric way. What our students learned from that tough and yet oddly gentle woman cannot be named. None of those who heard her speak is famous. I think it is a fairer test of our education that the student writers who listened to Miss Porter that afternoon would rather have emulated her than have won the Sophie Kerr Prize. Immodesty permitted, it might be a measure of our success as a college.

At Washington College, we have a small literary house: the O'Neill Literary House, named, not after the famous playwright, but after the mother of one of our most generous benefactors. It is our living verbal irony. In it you can find some of our better literary students. A few of those hold Sophie Kerr scholarships. They work away at reading books, writing papers and poems, composing short stories, giving readings of their work, editing magazines, publishing magazines. Some do nothing but read, write and think. The beauty of a good education is that it gives you a chance to be contemplative.

Those of us who teach these students have to remind ourselves—at times by looking at a list—who among them holds Sophie Kerr scholarships. They have declined to be even local heroes. I admire their solitude. But I worry about the day they will graduate and one of them will win a prize that is supposed, by its sheer bulk, to bring recognition. Nothing is the same after you take a picture of it.

I hope they can disappear back into their education and recall the insistent beauty of Elizabeth Bishop's poems, or the devout teaching Edward Albee once gave our drama students, or the great booming poetry reading of Joseph

Brodsky, or the gentle ambiance of the Rose O'Neill Literary House and the Washington College campus with its library stuffed with books yet to read.

In such nooks and crannies of college life is where the real prize glows. Maybe I shouldn't fear so strongly for my students: a good and generous education is the best shield they have against the mortality of fame.

"Print It As It Stands: Beautifully" –Henry James

This week, Washington College sent out invitations to its alumni and friends for a celebration and dedication next weekend of two recently acquired old Chandler and Price letterpresses and the lovely new letterpress room at the Rose O'Neill Literary House into which the letterpresses have been installed. Some must wonder what we are doing: why, in an age of technological fervor and a "communications explosion" is Washington College going backward—deliberately so, albeit in style. What, in the matters of liberal arts instruction, can be on our minds? Is our letterpress and its sunny room a museum? And what of the hundreds of thousands of pieces of type: Bodoni, Gothic, Cheltenham? And the old printer's shop tools: the composing stick, gauge pins, chases and cases? What has this lexicon to do with CRT's, computer disks, and megabytes? And then there is the question of time and how a college such as ours asks its students to spend time outside their first requirement of preparing for and attending classes. What are we doing with our letterpresses, anyway—much less celebrating them?

It is a Wednesday morning as I type this, and the Chandler and Price presses and the letterpress room are but thirty feet from me. They have the compelling solidity of an old train engine. When I turn the big one on for guests, I find myself saying, "Listen to the sound of the nineteenth century." My idea this morning was to compose a few lines of print for a longer text on which I am working. But I have a noon deadline to meet, and so I am typing it out on an Apple Macintosh 512K Enhanced, one of many word processors that are in the Literary House and scattered as well around the campus for use by students and faculty.

We are a networked college. By pushing certain buttons (I don't know which ones) I can connect myself to the great library at Dartmouth College and get a CTR full of bibliography on the history of printing. With my Apple, I can type out words, and if I don't like what they say, or how they say what is on my mind, there are two different buttons and one "mouse" I can use to rearrange or obliterate what I have written. I can store whole stories and bring them back to the screen, and unlike the galley I am filling in the letterpress room, it will not get dumped over and make what printers call "pie." Nor will I have to read it upside down. In fact, it will probably take two pressrooms to store in galleys what I can store on my Apple. Such are modern times, Charlie Chaplin keeps reminding me in the IBM ads.

Using the computer as a printer, the process of editing is in my machine, and while the process of thinking is still in my head, those of us who write for a living know all too well there is some mysterious connection between what we write and what we use to write—between what you think and what tools you've used to show what you think. In point of fact, if I were to set this article in the O'Neill Literary House pressroom using old printer's tools and my newfound, but amateurish, printer's skills, it would take me two days. You would be reading this the week after the pressroom celebration, and my deadline would not have been met. There is something to be said for that. Punctuality, Oscar Wilde once said, *is the thief of time*.

And it takes a certain attitude toward time to learn, if what you mean by learning is education, not training. What I have learned in recent weeks in the pressroom—and what the Washington College students now enrolled in the letterpress workshop we are offering are learning—is to take the time they need to print the words they want. A letterpress teaches you that because it can't be otherwise. You put in each letter at a time. With your fingers. You make corrections (a teaching colleague of mine set an entire poem backwards—a miscarried labor of love that took half the night to undo and do again, so it would be ready for the students' perusal in next morning's class) by hand, by fingers. The letterpress requires that you spend time with letters, with the type used to represent words, with the paper on which you choose to print poems and stories, with the ink, with the whole nine yards, as the students say. I wonder if it makes words worth more to the student who sets them in type than to the student who, like myself at this moment, flashes them onto a computer screen. I know that it is one of Washington College's missions to instruct students in the value of words: they are our link with our tradition. They *are* our tradition. We learn from both the word processor and the letterpress that the value of words has many perspectives.

It is true as well that what we learn when we set type is something about our literary cultural history. Students who have not discovered there is a link between language and previous arts and crafts are amused when our instructor points out the upper and lower cases, each filled with type, with the upper case placed, and filled with capital letters, above the lower one. Or that "rotogravure" is something more than a lyric in an old song their grandparents admired. We learn as well that our presses (circa 1914, 1949) are direct descendants of the Franklin press, which in turn is a direct descendant of the Gutenberg press—the press that gave us the Bible and the Protestant revolution of the sixteenth and seventeenth centuries. When asked in a recent survey to list significant turning points in modern history, American historians put the invention of the printing press first; second was the discovery of America.

But our group is a workshop, not a class at Washington College, and we wouldn't want to pretend that we study letterpress printing from a serious point of view on history or literature. That is not our object. We want to print. It fascinates us in some way that is difficult to explain, but that we all tend to understand. It makes for us the connection between art and craft and forges an understanding between the arts and crafts and the scholarship that examines the ideas that have grown out of such enterprises. Those of us who are writers share some understanding with other writers who have also been printers: Virginia Woolf and Walt Whitman. Yes, we are guilty of being romantic in our intellectual way about a job that required hard and often dirty work for little pay. We know about printer's thumbs, and we know about lost fingers and lead poisoning. We hope by our dabbling we don't demean the years of hard apprenticeship, or the centuries of difficult labor that is the history of letterpress printing. Rather, we hope we have the time to honor that tradition by doing good literary work—work that makes the word valuable in some way not easily understood by those of us who watch television. Marshall McLuhan observed that the printing press made readers of the public and that the Xerox machine made publishers of the public. The debate now to those of us interested in literary matters is which public is better. To have great poets, Whitman wrote, we need great audiences.

Perhaps it is the zeal that comes with discovery, but these days, I tend to think I prefer the value in words that comes out of the work and time it takes to set them in cold type. My colleague who set the poem backwards and then reset it correctly told me that when the students studied the poem in class, none of them wrote on it, taking their notes instead on a separate sheet of paper. Later some of them put it up on their dorm room walls. As teachers, our hope is that some relationship between the care we took in printing the poem and its intellectual value can be established. My own work (this article), edited by file menus, stored on disks, printed on laser printers, and put into offset newsprint for this weekend's edition, will get no such honor. Nor should it. Literary merit is a complex issue, and I don't mean to suggest that just printing something on the letterpress establishes it as worthy. But what I do mean to suggest is that Washington College's celebration of the letterpress is a celebration of close reading and careful work—as well as a celebration of an affection for a previous age. Besides, there is some intellectual fun to be had, and who wants to explain away the fun of it all: pica, quads, ink knife, free sheets, a kiss.

Allen Ginsberg Levitates Chestertown

Since the early 1970s, Chestertown has been host to hundreds of literary figures from all over the world, including scores of Pulitzer Prize and National Book Award winners, half a dozen or so Poet Laureates, plus four winners of the Nobel Prize in Literature: Toni Morrison, Joseph Brodsky, Derek Walcott, and J. M. Coetzee.

Among the other literary greats brought in by Washington College were the playwrights Edward Albee and Israel Horowitz; the French author Alain Robbe-Grillet; the poets William Stafford, Carolyn Forché, Henry Taylor, James Dickey, James Tate, Billy Collins, Dave Smith, and Lawrence Ferlinghetti; the Woody Allen screenplay writer Walter Bernstein; novelists Anthony Burgess, George Garrett, J. R. Salamanca; fiction writers such as William Gass, Mavis Gallant (of *New Yorker* fame), Joyce Carol Oates; plus our own William Warner, Chris Tilghman, Douglass Wallop, and John Barth. And that isn't the half of it. Just typing the list I realize I left off the poets Richard Wilbur, Donald Justice, Marvin Bell, Anthony Hecht, and Gwendolyn Brooks—as well as perhaps the finest American short-story writer of the twentieth century: Katherine Anne Porter.

Not all of these writers ventured into Chestertown for any length of time, but many of them did. I remember walking to the White Swan Tavern one day to pick up

Joseph Brodsky (he had come to Washington College with his translators, Anthony Hecht and Derek Walcott) and before I got there I found Derek Walcott browsing through the Compleat Bookseller. As I was early, I stopped in and Walcott talked a bit about the books he was buying (a copy of John Barth's *Letters* plus William Warner's *Beautiful Swimmers*).

Going out of the store, he asked me to walk him around town, and I did; he wanted to hear "apocryphal" stories of Chestertown and so I told him the one about how the local paper once carried the headline: "Baltimore Woman Dies at 92," referring to a woman who had come here when she was two and lived the rest of her life in town but, alas, was never considered a native by the natives. I told other tales as well, some of them irreverent and politically incorrect, and he seemed to like those best.

When we got back to the White Swan, Brodsky and Hecht were in a debate about some translation problem in one of Brodsky's poems and asked Walcott to settle it, which Walcott did by first looking at the Russian text of Brodsky's poem, then at Hecht's translation of the line, then at Brodsky's translation of the same line. After a moment Walcott fished a coin out of his pocket and flipped it: heads Anthony Hecht, tails Brodsky. Brodsky won. In such ways are Nobel Prize-winning poems translated by Nobel Prize-winning poets. On High Street in Chestertown, no less.

Later all four of us walked around, and the three of them recited various lines of Brodksy's poetry, sometimes in Russian, and then in various translations. When we got to the town dock, Walcott retold a few of the stories I had previously told him, and Brodsky recited a poem to the river. As it was in Russian, I had no notion why the Chester River should inspire the recitation of a poem, but it did: I do remember a waterman in his bateau looked at us, no doubt sure we were from "up to the College."

There were other writers who took time off from their duties at the College to walk into Chestertown. In the early seventies, William Stafford (the only poet to get an honorary degree from Washington College) wanted to see the Chester River, and at the town dock he also recited a few lines of poetry, this one (in English) being:

"What the river says, that is what I say," which is the final line of his famous poem "Ask Me."

A few years later Katherine Anne Porter and I were walking from the College to the home of Norman and Alice James for dinner when she wanted to know if we could get a bottle of Virginia Gentleman at the Past Time Bar; we could not, as it turned out, so she got it the next day on our way out of town. She did, however, stand me for "three fingers" of the "bar's best," and we arrived at the James's "refreshed"—to use Miss Porter's word.

But the most celebrated walk through Chestertown was taken by Allen Ginsberg and his lover Peter Orlofsky, followed by a dozen or so Washington College student poets: a peripatetic Aristotelian stroll through the heart of town.

The night before, Ginsberg had given a reading in the Norman James Theatre (spelled with the "re" that Norman James preferred). The place was packed, mainly with students and faculty, but with many people from Chestertown as well. At the reading Ginsberg read some of his more famous poems: "Howl" ("the best minds of my generation have gone mad"), "Supermarket in California" ("What thoughts I have of you tonight Walt Whitman"), "America" ("I'm putting my queer shoulder to the wheel"), but Ginsberg also read for the first time his now celebrated poem "Mind Breath," a poem that in its story circles the globe, starting that first night at Washington College, Chestertown, Maryland, and traveling through the times zones of the western United States, then on to Asia and Europe, to return to the podium from where he read. It was an astounding poem.

The next day Ginsberg and Orlofsky sat on the steps of the Richmond House (the Literary House of those days), talking about poetry. I remember Orlofsky had a guitar on which he would strum now and then in some relationship with whatever Allen Ginsberg was saying; I suppose it was a kind of emphasis, but I could never figure out a pattern.

After about an hour of talking with the students, Ginsberg got up and asked me if we might walk the campus and then through town. He wanted to levitate some of the buildings—both on the campus and off. "Sure," I said. The dean had recently admonished the faculty to provide "unique educational experiences" for our students, and I thought a building levitation might look good on my annual report. "Engaged learning," we now call it.

"Levitate whatever you want," I said.

"Can we watch?" asked one student.

"I'll bet you can't levitate Reid Hall," said a woman with red hair.

Off we went, Ginsberg leading us with Orlofsky among the students, strumming his guitar. Our first stop was the administration building, Bunting Hall.

With the students gathered behind them Ginsberg started a chant. "Ohmmmm. Ohmmmm. Ohmmmmmmmmmm." After a few moments when the building did not move, Ginsberg took small metal finger cymbals out of his pocket and, closing his eyes, rattled the cymbals and chanted with what seemed to me special vigor. "Ohmm! Ohmm! Ohmm!"

Still no movement of Bunting Hall.

"It is a very heavy building," said Ginsberg. "No doubt full of administrators."

"Let's go downtown," I said. "They've been talking about moving the old jail from in front of the courthouse and maybe you can help them."

"Lead on," said Orlofsky.

So off we all went down Mount Vernon Avenue, then took a right at Kent Street, a left at Calvert past the post office ("Very heavy buildings," said Orlofsky), through the park, then to the jail.

Ginsberg and Orlofsky looked at the jail for a moment. They left our group and went around to the side by Emmanuel Episcopal Church and looked at the jail from that angle. From where we were standing we could see they were in earnest conversation, no doubt discussing the best angle by which to raise the building—Orlofsky apparently wanting to pry it up from the side, but Ginsberg holding out for a full frontal floatation. They returned. By now a number of townspeople had gathered around our group.

"Where do they want it moved?" asked Ginsberg.

"Over by the railroad tracks," I said. "But I think they'd be grateful if you just got it off the ground because that would at least be a start."

"Jails are very heavy buildings," said Ginsberg. And then to Peter Orlofsky he started a spontaneous poetic chant (accompanied by Orlofsky on his guitar) enumerating the various jails into which one or the other of them—or both—had been tossed over the years. It was a splendid chant, and I wondered then if someday I might not see it in print as a poem. By this time I noticed that some of the men who were in the jail on the second floor had come to the windows to see what was going on.

"Maybe Reid Hall would be easier," said the young lady with the red hair. But by that time the chanting and finger cymbals and the guitar were in full swing: "Ohmmmmm! Ohmmmmmm. Ohm! Ohm. Ohmmmmmmmmmmmmmmm!"

It didn't work. For half an hour it didn't work. No jail moved. Maybe a hundred "Ohmmmms!" The jail stayed on the ground. The inmates seemed disappointed.

But in the end it seemed not to matter that the buildings of Washington College and Chestertown could not be levitated. There was the story of their not moving. The story of the chanting. The story of the walk back through town as Ginsberg recited Whitman's poetry and his own, speaking a line of his, and then a line of Whitman's, weaving an American poem a hundred years old and twenty years old at once. These stories were levitation in their own way.

Years later a student wrote me to claim the jail had in fact been raised by all the "Ohmmmmms." He could see it in his mind's eye, hovering above the ground, then easing down Cross Street toward the train station. The men in the jail were cheering as they went, as if to be in the air was to be free. I wondered what my student had been smoking that day.

The Myth Of Good College Teaching

At some point during the upcoming college graduation ceremonies there will be a moment when a member of the faculty is honored for excellence in classroom teaching. The chances are, even given local college politics, that the teacher deserves the recognition. That there is good college classroom teaching is not the myth: that it has any value in academic marketplace is. Think trading in rubles.

Consider my friend for 40 years, the brilliant American novelist John Barth. Over time I have met more than a few of his students from his Johns Hopkins teaching career. All of them praised the precision of his advice, his candor, his careful reading of their work. Yes. And because of who he was as an important novelist he held their attention with Coleridge's "glittering eye." And because of who he was he could have obtained distinguished professorships at a number of fine colleges and universities.

Now consider this: How about we create a doppelganger of John Barth albeit with few (if any) publications? Let us make him a teacher with deep knowledge of his subject, a teacher who prepares his classes with care. A teacher who is honored at graduation for his dedication to his students. And now let us imagine that this John Barth seeks the same professorships that the author of *The Floating Opera* (among many other novels) is seeking. Futility to the x times y power.

But of course John Barth's Hopkins students had the best of his glittering eye. Think about the well-published scholars and scientists in all academic fields, the specialists who are never going to be honored for their classroom teaching because they are neither good at it nor care much about it. Imagine they have won national and international prizes and awards far beyond their college and university. It doesn't take much to imagine that they too will get "the jobs, the dollars," to quote a line from W. D. Snodgrass' poem "April Inventory."

Each year I drive west on Interstate 70 from Chestertown, Md., to a remote town in northwestern Kansas, and along the way I see billboards advertising universities and colleges: One school claims a celebrated basketball player starred on its team; a small college asserts that it has a business program that will get its students jobs; a state school announces it is a nationally recognized "Research University"; another college brags that a famous speech had been given there; and (my favorite) a university shows a massive picture of two clenched bare-knuckled fists sporting 10 championship rings from various NCAA playoffs. Taken together, these billboards are 15 minutes of fame for the colleges and universities that line the interstate highways of America (well, 15 seconds at 70 mph).

To be fair, you can't put a picture of a celebrated teacher on a billboard (who would pay the bill? Not the athletic department), nor would any good teacher want that: *Praise to the face is open disgrace*, as the old rule would have it. And if you were an honored teacher, you would probably not want to be celebrated at the half-time ceremony of a football game—something I once witnessed.

So what's to be done? Not much as it turns out. There is of course satisfaction in itself from teaching well; not unlike the pleasure of learning is the pleasure of learning—thus a liberal arts education, also not a valued currency.

Or there is this, again from "April Inventory":

There is a gentleness survives
That will outspeak and has its reasons.
There is a loveliness exists,
Preserves us, not for specialists.

Tales Of Retirement

Those of us who stop teaching at colleges and universities have our stories. This is Professor Nick Newlin, Chairman of my English Department at Washington College, circa 1973.

"Bob, I can no longer hear the young ladies in my class."

We are alone in the faculty lounge.

"What do you hear?" I ask.

"I hear them peep."

"Peep?"

"I call on them and they go peep, peep, peep in their tiny voices. When they stop, I say, 'Very interesting.'"

"Worse things have been said," I say.

"No doubt," Nick says. "We are in a dubious business, talking about what the students can learn as well from reading books."

Not long afterwards Nick retired, and his gift to our seniors was his elegant commencement address of that year. We heard every word.

Some of my colleagues did not get to retire. Professor Norman James, Nick Newlin's successor as English Department chairman, died absurdly in his professorial prime. But I remember a faculty meeting not long before his death where we learned our college had received a modest grant for audio-visual aids: Did anyone, the dean asked, have suggestions about how to spend the funds? After a moment's silence, Norman said that new erasers in the William Smith classrooms would be helpful, and if there was enough money, we might put in a supply of good chalk against hard times. No one had a better idea.

Later in the same meeting Norman was asked why the English Department did not teach comparative literature. "Because," he thundered, "we teach superlative literature." I suspect had Norman lived to see the day when he was invited to attend a Power Point workshop so he might better teach Yeats' "When You Are Old and Grey," he would have considered it a herald to stop his superlative brand of teaching.

Nor did Professor Mike Bailey, my colleague in the Economics Department, have a chance to retire. But I recall his coming into the faculty lounge one day and, observing a cluster of senior faculty engaged in earnest conversation, pronouncing the Bailey Theorem: *Where two or more full professors are gathered together, they are doubtless talking about their retirement portfolios*. To which he added the Bailey Corollary: *The stock market goes up until it goes down. Then it goes down until it goes up.*

More recently Professor Al Briggs of our Math Department retired after thirty-five years of always returning his calculus exams in the class after he had given them. Then one day, he forgot. When he remembered, he remembered not only had he forgotten to return the exams, he remembered he had forgotten to grade them, and then he remembered he had forgotten he had ever given them. With these x's and y's on the tally sheet before him, Al calculated it was time to retire before he forgot to do so. And so he did.

As for myself, there was the student who wrote on my teacher-evaluation form that because I was the only politically incorrect professor left at the college, he thought it best to take my American Literature course before I was arrested.

Then this: At the end of a class, I noticed a young lady in her seat after all others had left.

"May I help you? I asked. She said something that sounded vaguely like peep, peep—after which she got up and walked toward me, Julia in her clothes, all lithe and lovely.

"I want to hug you," she said.

"Me?" I said, standing straighter while trying to deflate my inner-tube girth. "Me?"

"Yes," she said.

I looked for hidden cameras. Before I could reply, she said, "It's just that you remind me so much of my grandfather."

Epilogue

from Berryman

I asked how you can ever be sure
that what you write is really
any good at all and he said you can't

you can't you can never be sure
you die without knowing
whether anything you ever wrote was any good
if you have to be sure don't write

— W.S. Merwin

Afterword

Education—the kind that goes on in classrooms—takes many forms. One is imparting specific information: irregular Spanish verbs, the capitals of Europe, names of the bones in the human skeleton. Another is introducing concepts: the side-angle-side postulate, ethnocentrism, Frederick Jackson Turner's Frontier Thesis. Still another is modeling an attitude of inquiry: demonstrating by example the curiosity, discipline, and techniques that make it possible to learn more about the subject at hand. After three decades of teaching, I've come to believe that while the first two are important, the third is the most valuable, the one that will encourage any given semester's students to be lifelong students. There are as many ways to model that attitude as there are good teachers, but what they all share is passion, which Bob Day had—and after visiting with him a few months back, I can attest, still has.

It's been 35 years since I was a student in one of Bob Day's classes, but I remember it as if it were, well, a few days before yesterday. Our first meeting was actually by phone: I had applied to Washington College, and when I indicated an interest in creative writing, I was encouraged to submit a sample manuscript. A few days after I mailed it off, I was awakened by a phone call (to be fair: the call may have come at noon. Like a lot of teenagers, I was a dedicated sleeper.). Bob Day, sitting in his office in Chestertown, proceeded to do what he must have done for many hundreds of prospective students over the years: he (somehow) found something to praise in the work; he suggested, kindly, a few specific ways it might be improved; he named a few books I should read; and he made it clear that this was the sort of attention I could expect to get for four years, if I chose to make my way from suburban Baltimore to the Eastern Shore.

All told, I believe I enrolled in five or six of his classes at Washington College, because they were what constituted the college's unofficial creative writing program at the time. Most of the classes were workshops, but at least one was a literature course focused on the American short story.

To say Bob was an enthusiastic, engaged teacher would be accurate but insufficient. He managed to be both absolutely serious about introducing us to fine fiction and poetry—by writers as varied as W. S. Merwin, Katherine Anne Porter, John Cheever, Gwendolyn Brooks, Tim O'Brien, William Gass, Mavis Gallant, John Ashbery, Donald Hall, James Dickey, Edward Albee, and Toni Morrison (most of whom he brought to campus to talk with us)—and about as playful as a college professor can be and stay employed. He made writing poetry and fiction seem as important a thing as one could dedicate one's time to, as well as a great amount of fun. He brought Allen Ginsberg in to discuss our poetry (Ginsberg, to me: "Is this a poem?"), the editor of *The Atlantic Monthly* in to discuss our fiction (C. Michael Curtis, to me: "This is not a story."). He instituted The Broken Chalk Award—if one of us correctly answered a particularly difficult or obscure question, he'd snap a stick of chalk in half and toss it across the room to the honoree who, nearly always to his or her surprise, caught it—and kept body counts of the numbers of people killed in the goriest student stories. But he also taught us about character and image, simile and metaphor, and the pleasures of a well-turned sentence.

And Nabokov. Always, Nabokov. Bob routinely screened the filmed interview he describes in one of these essays, and a letter from Vera (thanking the writers of Washington College for their expression of birthday wishes to the man himself) was prominently displayed just inside Richmond House, the dilapidated, eventually condemned building that served as the College's first home for student writers, as well as Bob's office. That alone tells you something: while other faculty, quite understandably, had their offices in classroom buildings or buildings dedicated to faculty offices, Bob always chose to be surrounded by students. For that matter, he seemed to believe all writers shared his enthusiasm for undergraduates. These days, when esteemed writer X shows up on a college or university campus, there's an excellent chance he or she will spend a good deal of time with other professors, or administrators, or even donors. Writers visiting Washington College were in the company of students from the time they landed at the airport until they made their escape. It was heady stuff. (Bob, to me, in his office one afternoon: "Who should we bring to campus next spring?" Me: "Joseph Heller." Bob reaches for phone.) And if the distance between our work and that of the writers with whom we had meals, played wiffle ball, and even, once, went to church was much greater than any of them let on, the message was clear: these people whose writing we admire are not so different from you and me. You can be one of them, if you dedicate yourself to it.

As is evident in these essays, Bob is a mythmaker. He told us he came from a place called Kansas. I'm well aware that there's an actual place called Kansas; I've been there, and it bears little or no resemblance to the place Bob talks and writes about. Actual Kansas is fairly ordinary, running toward dull; Bob's Kansas is full of wit and charm, with touches of sadness and wisdom. Bob Day's Kansas, like the world of writing he created for all of his students, is a place you want to visit; and if it turns out not to be somewhere you can actually live, the striving to get there can be awfully rewarding.

— Peter Turchi

Acknowledgements

The author notes with pleasure the precise editorial advice by Steve Hill, associate editor of the *University of Kansas Alumni Magazine* where many of the pieces were published, as well as the gifted design work of Diane Landskroener plus the clerical assistance of Cathy Naundorf and Cindy Licata.

This volume of *Learning and Teaching* also honors the establishment of the Barbara and George Cromwell Center For Teaching and Learning at Washington College, where students and teachers discuss the subjects addressed herein.

Author's Notes

Robert Day's novel *The Last Cattle Drive* was a Book-of-the-Month Club selection. His short fiction has won a number of awards and citations, including two Seaton Prizes, a PEN/Faulkner NEA prize, and Best American Short Story and Pushcart citations. His fiction has been published by *Tri-Quarterly, Black Warrior Review, Kansas Quarterly, North Dakota Quarterly, Summerset Review,* and *New Letters* among other belles-lettres magazines. He is the author of two novellas, *In My Stead,* and *The Four Wheel Drive Quartet,* as well as three collections of short fiction: *Speaking French in Kansas, Where I Am Now,* and *The Billion Dollar Dream.*

His nonfiction has been published in the *Washington Post Magazine, Smithsonian Magazine, Forbes FYI, Modern Maturity, World Literature Today, American Scholar,* and *Numero Cinq.* As a member of the Prairie Writers Circle, his essays have been reprinted in numerous newspapers and journals nationwide, and on such internet sites as *Counterpunch* and *Arts and Letters Daily.* Recent book publications include *We Should Have Come By Water* (poems), *The Committee to Save the World* (literary non-fiction), *Chance Encounters of a Literary Kind* (memoirs), and *Let Us Imagine Lost Love* (a novel).

Among his awards and fellowships are a National Endowment for the Arts Creative Writing Fellowship,

Yaddo and McDowell fellowships, a Maryland Arts Council Award, and the Edgar Wolfe Award for distinguished fiction. His teaching positions include The Iowa Writers Workshop; The University of Kansas; and the Graduate Faculty at Montaigne College, The University of Bordeaux.

He is past Acting President of the Associated Writing Programs; the founder and former Director of the Rose O'Neill Literary House; and founder and Publisher of the Literary House Press at Washington College, Chestertown, Maryland.

Barbara A. Mowat is Director of Research Emerita at the Folger Shakespeare Library, Consulting Editor of *Shakespeare Quarterly*, and Editor (with Paul Werstine) of the New Folger Library Shakespeare. She holds an M.A. degree in English literature from the University of Virginia, a Ph.D. in English literature from Auburn University, and Doctorates of Humane Letters from Amherst College, St. Johns University, and Washington College. Before coming to the Folger, she was Hollifield Professor of English Literature at Auburn University and then Dean of the College at Washington College. She has served as President of the Shakespeare Association of America, President of the Southeast Renaissance Conference, Chair of the MLA Committee on the New Variorum Shakespeare, and a member of the Advisory Board of the International Shakespeare Conference (Stratford-upon-Avon).

Peter Turchi is the author of six books, including *A Muse and a Maze: Writing as Puzzle, Mystery, and Magic,* and *Maps of the Imagination: The Writer as Cartographer.* He is also the co-editor of three anthologies. The recipient of fellowships from the National Endowment for the Arts and the John Simon Guggenheim Foundation, North Carolina's Sir Walter Raleigh Award, and Washington College's Sophie Kerr Prize; he currently teaches at the University of Houston and in the MFA Program for Writers at Warren Wilson College.